A Place to Call Home

A Place to Call Home

DR. MAXINE ELM

PALMETTO
P U B L I S H I N G
Charleston, SC
www.PalmettoPublishing.com

Paperback ISBN: 979-8-8229-5417-5
eBook ISBN: 979-8-8229-5418-2

Contents

Chapter One

"Small days is still on my mind"
Growing up in Guyana, South America

"Oh beautiful Guyana, oh my lovely native land more dear to me than all the world thy sea-washed, sun-kissed strand, or down upon the waters looking out upon the deep, the great Atlantic blown into a fury or asleep at morn at noon or better in the crimson's sunset glow. I love thee, oh I love thee." Valerie Rodway, Walter Macarthur Lawrence, "Beautiful Guyana", year unknown.

It was February 21st, 1975 on a bright and sunny morning in New Amsterdam, Berbice, Guyana when I was born. I grew up in a small apartment in the Savannah Park Housing Scheme (also known as the first scheme). The first scheme "passay" as it was fondly called was a tightly knitted community and everybody was considered family; it was one big extended, blended family. The children cooked, ate, and played together and the elders looked out for every one. It truly took a village to raise children in those days. The elders would whoop any child in the neighborhood caught misbehaving and when they told your parents you would get another whooping. Children had respect for their elders and regarded them as their aunts and uncles; all the elders in the community were referred to as auntie or uncle. During the afternoons we would play various childhood games and at nights the children would gather around to listen to the elders tell fairytales or what we called Nancy stories. Weekends would be spent cooking in the bushes with stoves made from tinning cups and wood; we called it bush cook. We would cook rice, curried mango, fry bush fish (fishes we would catch from the trenches), or anything else our parents had in their pantry at home. It truly took a village because everybody regarded and looked out for each other as though they were family even though not related by blood. During the summer months, I would travel to Ebini Berbice River to visit my paternal grandparents. My cousins and I would walk the pasture, pick and eat fruits from the trees, go fishing, and swim in the Berbice River for countless hours or paddle around in canoes visiting other relatives. In those days Guyana's waters were unchartered, there was no oil discovery or multistory malls, fast food chains, and hotels with casinos, there was a uniqueness, a quiet sense of peace, and a general sense of satisfaction with life. Going to Georgetown was a special occasion, eating food from the Chinese restaurant was a treat, and a visit to Demico Quik Serve was a special and exciting trip. Attending school tours, sports, and fairs were special occasions, everybody would get dressed in their Sunday best and ready to shine during those events. Walking back and forth to Berbice High school with your crew of friends with friendly banter and laughter was a daily routine.

It was the era of rubber band and marble competition, jumping the neighbors' fences after school to pick fruits; walking on the dam to pick up water nuts, cracking them with our teeth and eating them on our way home. On the weekends feeling for fishes and swimming in the nearby trenches, cleaning and frying bush fish was our adventure. Gata, Lawah, tamarind balls, pickled mango and plantain chips with sour were our every day snacks. When no one was in the kitchen we would steal milk powder from the can and eat it with sugar and make sure to wipe our mouths clean so we don't get a whooping for stealing food. Eating dry coconut and sugar was a thing, I still eat it to this day. Fruits were in abundance, we would have sapodillas, star apples, awara, mangoes and genips whenever they were in season. We drank lime drink or what was called swank and cool aid drinks, there was no soda or pop. Our parents would give us money to buy icicles and flutie from the people that sell them and we would buy snow cone from the snow cone carts when they passed through the neighborhood. We drank water straight from the tap and never worried about getting sick. We ride bicycles without helmets and never had a head injury. We played in the streets without shoes and wasn't worried about harming ourselves. There was no computer or cell phones we knocked on each other's doors when we wanted to find other children. There were no guns and knives being used during fights. We had fist fights and if all else failed pelting someone with a brick and running home was the next best option. While playing in the streets every once in awhile we would run into our homes or the closest home to wherever we were playing in the neighborhood to drink water out of the tap and go back to playing. Whenever the rain fell we would play and take showers in the rain. The community was an extended family in every sense of what an extended family represents, there was genuine care and concern for each other.

Growing up in Guyana we lived a humble life, we were poor, had to share our beds with our siblings, and didn't have everything we wanted but we always had everything we needed. We never went to bed hungry, we always had clothes on our backs and shoes on our feet. We had no choice in what we ate, we had to eat what our parents cooked. There was one television in the home and two television stations Christie and Vieira. We would all gather together at night to watch WWE wrestling and debate on who the winner of the match would be. We hung out with our cousins and huddled together in chairs and couches or on mattresses on the floor to sleep. The relationship we had as cousins was close we would play ludo and snake on ladder among other games and were inseparable. We would venture into SandVoort on the weekends to drink coconut water, eat sugar cane, catch fish, and swim in the black water trenches. Those were the days when the family stood on Unity and the family bond was strong. In those days when one family member stumped their toe the entire family felt the pain. My mother was a grassroots politician so she was always busy, my eldest sister would run the house in my mother's absence or we would spend the night by one of my aunt's homes. My mother was a strict disciplinarian and she was famous for giving whoopings. My mother's weapons of choice would be anything within her hand's reach; pot spoons, pots, shoes, or any weapon of destruction she could find. My mother's nick name growing up was "karate ya, ya" because she whooped first and then asked questions later. Whenever one person was getting a whooping every other child in the home would be scared because they knew that their turn was coming. She would beat you for things you did weeks prior whenever she get to sharing whoppings.

Our family was religious so morning devotions were routine, every Friday when the sun set we would welcome the sabbath and Saturday would be spent in church worshipping. I wanted to learn how to play the piano and would go to piano lessons at the church twice a week. All the children in the family were taught how to pray and had to memorize memory verses from the bible to recite during morning devotion or when the family welcomed the sabbath. My mom cooked and prepared all the dishes for Saturday on Friday evening since there was no cooking allowed on Saturday. As children we were actively involved in pathfinders and master guides clubs at the church. We would go away to different camping events, and participate in parades and club competitions. My mother was very strict and did not compromise with it came to the sabbath and going to church, you had to go to church unless you were ill.

Growing up in Guyana built the foundation of hard work, working for everything you need, and learning the importance of independence and self-efficacy. High school days were a mixture of growing up and taking on adult responsibilities; learning the importance of waking up on time so you are not late for school, getting dressed, and arriving at school before the first bell rang because whenever you arrived late for school Mr. Nankisore would be waiting for you at the school gate and the consequences were not pleasant. In addition to the whooping, you had to clean the school compound, the embarrassment was worse than the actual task. On days I would get to school late I would approach the school gate very slowly and always contemplated turning around and going back home because I didn't want to deal with Mr. Nankisore's punishment but when I thought of going back home and dealing with my mom, I would rather deal with Mr Nankisore's beating than my mother's. Learning home economics, the basics of cooking, cleaning, and performing household tasks was beneficial in preparing me for adulthood. The five years in high school went by quickly and before I knew it I was getting ready to take the Caribbean examination Council (CXC) examinations the examination all students take when exiting high school. After completing high school at age 17, I applied for and obtained my first job as a teacher at Viola Nursery School. I spent the next three years teaching and attending Cyril Potter College of Education studying to become a certified teacher. It was three months before graduation when I received my visa for permanent residency in the United States of America and subsequently left Guyana shortly after. My final days at Viola Nursery and in Guyana were sad; I was leaving my students and colleagues behind and also leaving Guyana and life as I had known for the past twenty years in search of a new home, with no idea of what the future holds for me. I was about to venture into unchartered waters with no idea of what life would be like over yonder. In those days most people were excited to leave the shores of Guyana, they held celebratory parties with their friends and family, there was this perception that life overseas was better and going to the United States of America was an escape from poverty and the simple life Guyana offered at the time; it was an opportunity to build wealth and enjoy the finer things in life. In my situation there was nothing to celebrate, anxiety and fear plagued me for weeks before my departure, I didn't sleep well at night and as it got closer to the time for me to leave I became more sad and started missing home even before I left. I still remember the morning I boarded the minibus for Timehri International airport accompanied by my mother and siblings. It was a somber ride there was this eerie silence and it felt like I was slowly making my way to the hanging chamber and was about to enjoy my last supper. The minibus made its way through the country side I was staring out the window at all the fruit trees and admiring the careless swaying of the coconut trees, I was taking in every last drop of this familiar scenery. After about two hours we arrived at the airport. Saying good bye is never easy we were all crying, it was a sad moment especially for me because I was leaving not for a brief vacation with the intention of returning home shortly, I was leaving home with no idea if and when I would be returning. I was leaving my beautiful country Guyana, it was surreal, I sat at the airport lounge waiting to board my flight and could not stop my mind from wondering. I sat there longing to cross the Berbice River with the Torani again, already missing the weekend adventures to Sandvoort with my cousins, unsure if I would ever be able to sit on the stairs with my step dad and hear him tell my favorite stories, I just wanted to walk back through the doors of Viola Nursery school and teach one more lesson but instead I was being called to board this white iron bird, it was happening, this wasn't a dream I was actually leaving home.

Chapter Two

America: Bed of roses or crown of thorns

*E*xactly one week before my 21st birthday I left the shores of Guyana on a Caribbean Airlines flight bound for Trinidad and Tobago where I had to connect to my flight bound for New York. I had my yellow envelope in hand and was accompanied by my sister. It was my first time on an airplane and my first time leaving Guyana. I was assigned a window seat and as the airplane rose above ground I looked out at Guyana's lush greenery and tears rolled down my cheeks. I had mixed emotions, I was leaving the only home I knew for the last twenty years and was venturing into the unknown. A new country, a new way of life, and going to live with a father I barely knew. I felt overwhelmed with anxiety and the feeling of sadness, I sobbed uncontrollably until the airplane disappeared into a bed of clouds and there was no trace of Guyana in sight.

Forty-five minutes later we touched down at Piarco airport in Trinidad. There was a massive snowstorm in New York the previous day and our flight was delayed so we had to spend the night in Trinidad and wait to get on our connecting flight to New York the next morning. The airline housed us in a hotel for the night and I laid there the entire night unable to sleep. My heart was racing, my thoughts were wondering, tears periodically streaming down my face; every few hours I would walk to the room window and gaze at the stars twinkling in the blackness of the night, this will be the closest I will get to home for a long time. The next morning, we boarded our flight for New York and reality started to set in; I was on my way, and there was no turning back. After about 4 hours the pilot announced our final descent into John J Kennedy airport, New York. I was trying hard to reason with myself at this point, I was going to find a better life but at the same time I felt like a lamb being led to slaughter, it was bittersweet.

After clearing immigration my sister and I headed out to meet my cousin who was waiting for us with jackets in hands, as we exited all I could see was piles of snow everywhere and the blast of cold winter air hit my face, I came face to face with winter for the first time. I spent the night wrapped up in thick blankets, afraid to use the restroom because I didn't want to leave the warmth of the bed. The next morning we would be leaving for California, our final destination, my new place to call home. As the sun started to rise and morning approached my anxiety level started to rise again, during the flight my nerves were getting the best of me, I started feeling nauseous and was vomiting, I could hear the thumping of my heartbeat as my heart continued to race out of my chest. I was getting a tension headache and feelings of intermittent dizziness. After five-plus hours we touched down at LAX in Los. Angeles, California. After landing we went to baggage claim to uplift our bags and while waiting for our bags I was silently praying that God would help me to control my anxiety before I met my dad. If there was one thing my mother taught me was to pray when the odds are against me.

We collected our bags and headed towards the exit where my dad was waiting for us. It was a long ride from Los Angeles to Perris, Riverside. I sat in the car and tried to process the new environment. The buildings were extremely tall and the traffic was thick. I had never seen that number of vehicles before so I was in awe. The multiple fast food restaurants, the lights, the hustling and bustling of the city, and the horrific traffic were far-fetched from life in small town, New Amsterdam, Berbice, and Guyana. In my hometown there were no traffic lights, you could count the number of cars passing you on the road on any given day, there were no fast food chains and long stretch of cars moving at snail's pace on the freeway. My thoughts were, "father please how would a country girl like me ever adjust to life in this big city?!

Two hours later we arrived in Perris to my father's home, our new home. I was exhausted and just wanted to go to bed. I changed my clothing, laid down, said my prayers, and tried my best to fall asleep, the time difference took some adjusting to so I was wide awake at 3 AM just staring at the ceiling, thoughts wandering, anxiety level mounting, and still silently praying to the almighty for calmness. Days passed and then weeks, I was missing Guyana and home but trying my best to adjust. Over the weeks while trying to adjust many things started to unfold. I was 21 years old and I had lost my independence, I had no job, no money, no car, and no autonomy to make any decision on my own, I was dependent on others some because of my circumstances and others by mandate. I could no longer make any decision on what I ate, what I wore, or where I went. I felt like a 21-year-old adult forced to assume the identity and mannerisms of a 14-year-old child. I had to be mindful of what I said, what I wore, and where I went, my every action was monitored and controlled. How does a 21-year-old adult adjust to this new life, in this new place that I am supposed to call home, under these circumstances? My life was miserable, I spent many nights crying in silence, angry, feeling hopeless, and worthless, and trying to make sense of everything that was happening.

As my anger grew so did my rebelliousness and it was evident in my frequent outbursts; the environment was contentious, and the disagreements were many and frequent. There was no compromise, no reasoning or rationalization it was strictly "our way or the highway", "our house our rules". At twenty-one years old I had no input in anything about my life or everyday wellbeing. Imagine being hurt and unable to cry because you would be told not to shed "crocodile tears." I had to read a book and tell the story to get five dollars or wash a vehicle to earn ten dollars. All my underclothing, deodorant, lotions, or makeup had to come from an Amway catalog otherwise I wasn't allowed to have it. My grandfather bought me a pair of Fila sneakers from the mall once and that resulted in a very condescending verbal scolding.

In the months right after coming from Guyana, we moved from Perris to Santa, Maria, California. I got my first job working at the McDonalds' on the other side of town about 4 miles from home. I worked for minimum wage and only worked part time about twenty hours a week so I made limited money. I had no driver's license or no car so I had to rely on the bus that only worked certain hours or ride the second-hand bicycle that one of my aunts gave me. The bicycle was old and the tires would puncture often so many days I would have to push the bicycle from the job to the house because the tires were flat and I couldn't ride it. You had to be mindful of what you ate, since some of the food in the refrigerator was off-limits, life was rough. This was the epiphany of a culture shock but in the worst way.

My anger continued to mount and it was affecting my attitude, and causing a lot of conflicts. Amidst all of the chaos I longed for home and my humble beginning in small town, New Amsterdam; I felt homeless, I existed in a house that I could not call home, it was the place where I ate and slept but there was no sense of belonging, this was not home. The house was contentious and I knew it wouldn't be long before this situation came to an end, either by me voluntarily leaving or being asked to involuntarily leave with my bags thrown out on the street, something had to give, and hastily. I had two choices either go back home to Guyana or go somewhere else and try to start over. I had to make a decision and do something quickly before something drastic happened. If I decided to go back to Guyana I would have to buy my ticket since I had forfeited the one-way ticket that was bought to send me back to Guyana some months ago. If I decided to go somewhere else I needed to be able to buy an airline ticket and have some money to survive. I couldn't allow myself to be consumed with self-pity I had to get up and get. As the days went by I was talking with my mother and a friend I had in New York trying to figure it out. My mother didn't want me to go back to Guyana because I had come here in search of a better life and she felt going back to Guyana would defeat that purpose. So after some days, the decision to go to New York was made. My bags were packed and I was heading to LAX once again to embark on another journey in search of a place to call home. This time was different though, all my dreams of the bed of roses had vanished and now my journey was different because this time I was wearing a crown of thorns; I was mentally and emotionally scarred and full of anger and hatred. Unlike the day I left Guyana, there were no bitter-sweet moments I was just bitter. I was broke, with no plan for the future and no place to go but it didn't matter, in my mind sleeping on the streets would have been more peaceful that abiding in a home full of contention and strife. I was on my way to face the music of what it would feel like to be in a strange place with no support system, it was time to fend for myself.

Chapter Three

New York City - The big apple
(sweet, sour, or rotten to its core)

After 5 hours on a United Airlines flight, I touched down at LaGuardia airport in New York city, to begin my life in the big apple. I had two hundred dollars in my pocket, no job, and about twelve outfits in a bag most of them not winter-appropriate in the middle of winter, nevertheless, I was determined to make it work, I had no choice I had to do it. I had nothing but I was hopeful because I had my freedom. There would be no more frequent conflicts, I could finally be an adult and have autonomy over my life and decisions, I felt free; tonight I could finally lay down and not cry myself to sleep in silence. The next morning was the dawn of a new day, I had to learn my way around New York City, find a job, and try to make life and find a home here. New York had plenty of public transportation and it was easy to get around either by bus or train at any time. My first job in New York city was at the Toys' R Us on Flatbush Avenue pass the Kings Plaza Mall. I would take the city bus to Kings Plaza and then walk about 1 mile to the store. On the nights I had to close I would have to walk from the store to Kings Plaza after 10 pm to take the bus home, it would be dark and cold and I would be praying the entire way until I got to the bus stop. Life in New York City was challenging, I had to take many odds and ends minimum wage jobs to survive because I had no college education or skill. The Toys r Us job was seasonal so when the Christmas season ended that job also came to an end. After that I took a part time job at Shea stadium, where the New York Mets played baseball and that was also only available during baseball season. I couldn't use my high school diploma from Guyana because it was in a different last name, I had to get a GED. For the first two years living in New York City, I had no permanent place of abode, I was either renting rooms in people's houses or living with relatives and friends. I remember being at a friend's home and they had some visitors from Guyana; one of the visitors asked where I lived and their daughter said she was homeless; she didn't have a home. While renting a room there was a time that I could not pay the rent the landlord's husband came into the room one night at midnight and tried to rape me, I left that night and went to the subway station at McDonald Avenue and slept there until the next morning before going to a friend's house.

Staying at other people's houses always comes with challenges. In some instances, I slept on sofas in people's living rooms because they didn't have an extra bedroom I could occupy. I was working for minimum wage and had to contribute to the household from the little money I got paid. I had to be mindful of what I took out of their refrigerator and would have to eat after everybody else ate. I had to be in the house before a certain time because I didn't have a key to the front door and would have to sleep outside. While working at Shea stadium in Queens I would be running every evening after work to make sure I didn't miss the train that came at a specific time because I didn't want to get locked out and have to sleep in the apartment lobby. I had a few pieces of clothing that I would recycle on a weekly basis, but it didn't matter to me once they were clean. I had one pair of sneakers that I would wear during the winter as well as the summer months because I couldn't afford to buy winter boots. I had a secondhand winter jacket that was given to me by one of my cousins and I wore it every winter for years until I could afford to buy a new winter jacket. Those days I didn't own a cell phone and would have to use the pay phones on the streets to communicate with others. The first couple of years in New York City I was living from hand to mouth, I was barely surviving on the salary I made and I was living from paycheck to paycheck. Some days I would eat one meal because I couldn't afford three meals. I had no support system so I had to make it work by myself. I was struggling and many days I contemplated on going back to Guyana but I didn't even have money to afford a one way ticket back to Guyana, so I had to stay in New York and make it work somehow. Life was rough many days I would cry by myself because I couldn't share my struggles with anyone. I only trusted a few people and even some of those people betrayed my trust. Some of the people I trusted to confide in not only made me into a mocking stock but shared my story with other people so that they can talk derogatory about me as well. I didn't have a beeper or cell phone or anything so I would have to use the pay phones on the street corners to communicate with others. I had few friends so I spent most of my time talking to the almighty, telling him everything that I was going through, I was going through tough times but I knew one day things would change I just had to keep the faith and continue fighting. Prayer, faith and hope kept me alive and pushing, I took my best friend Jesus with me every where I went, I was learning the importance of trusting him where I could not trace him and I was thankful that my momma taught me how to pray when the odds were against me. I prayed and fought my way out of many battles some too daring to repeat. It is so easy for people to criticize and speak on your reaction to situations and things but nobody understand your pain and the many dark places you had to fight your way out of. If you don't know someone's struggles you shouldn't speak on their decisions because only the person wearing the shoes can feel the pain from walking in it.

One day while reading the newspaper I saw a hiring advertisement for Century 21 store in Manhattan, I took the train to the store, applied for a job and was hired. It was during one of the times that I stayed at a family friend's house that I met my husband. After dating for sometimes we moved in together in a one bedroom basement in Richmond Hill, Queens. We lived there for sometime before moving into a two bedroom apartment in Jamaica, Queens, I was taking the train into Manhattan to go to work. While working at century 21 department store as a cashier one of my colleagues who was going to school to become a medical assistant encouraged me to apply to go to school to become a medical assistant, which I subsequently did. After 12 months I graduated as a medical assistant and got a job at New York Presbyterian hospital in their outpatient OB/GYN department where I spent five years working. During those five years, I got married and had my first child, my son Mekhi. When my son was about five months old I went back to school to become a nurse. I worked Monday through Friday 8 to 4 PM and went to nursing school on nights and weekends while my mom baby sat my son. I would be on the train late at night going home, tired sometimes falling asleep, and passing my stop on the train. My mother would stay up with me at night quizzing me on content for my examinations. During nursing school the first separation of my now ex-husband occurred, we were having marital problems and he left and went to live in Trinidad. I was struggling to take care of my son and continue to attend nursing school. After about a year my husband took my son to stay with him in Trinidad while I completed my nursing degree. Long Island Jewish Hospital gave me my first nursing job on the neurology unit on the night shift. After a few months of starting my job at LIJ my husband and son returned to the United States and our life as a family continued. In March 2009, I gave birth to my second child a baby girl. Life in New York was turning the corner for the better, I was starting to taste some of the sweet of the big apple. New York was finally starting to feel like a place I could call home

Chapter Four

The L's and the D:
Love, lost and divorce

It was the summer of 1997 when I met my now ex-husband. I was staying at one of our family friend's resident in Brooklyn and he came to visit, they were his cousins. It started off as friendly banter, then over a period of time grew into dating and eventually a relationship. We lived together for some years; first in Richmond Hill, Queens then we subsequently moved to Jamaica, Queens. Like with every relationship there were good and bad times. We were both good people but not necessarily good for each other, we both had our flaws and sometimes we struggle to find common ground on the most basic of things. I was young, naïve, stubborn and had difficulty trusting people. I had a lot of unhealed wounds and I was definitely bleeding on innocent people. We both worked hard to ensure the bills were paid. The first five years of being together was rough on the both of us but we still had some good times. On the weekend I would accompany my ex husband to cheer him on as he played cricket and we would often drive over to Newark, New Jersey to eat at the restaurants, walk along Broad street to the various stores and shop from Bobby's department store and Save-A-thon among other stores. We would go on bus rides to the casino in Connecticut and the shopping outlets in Redding, Pennsylvania. Those were the good times before we had children and before our differences became irreconcilable. We worked hard on making our home a place that we could come home after a hard day's work and relax we made sure it had every needed amenity. Over those years I got pregnant twice; I had a stillborn at 20 weeks and then a miscarriage at 8 weeks. The doctors were convinced that I could not have normal, viable pregnancies due to have been diagnosed with PCOS and hormonal imbalances. There was always that possibility that I would never be able to conceive and carry a healthy baby to term. Nevertheless, we continued on with our lives and relationship. After being together for about five years we went to the court house and got married, no fancy ceremony or anything and no celebration after the fact; we signed our papers in the presence of one of our close friend and came home and continued our lives as per normal, nothing had changed. Then the unexpected pregnancy came and it brought many challenges with it. I was suffering from hyperemesis gravida in my first trimester and was in and out of the hospital for IV hydration due to rapidly losing weight and consistent vomiting. The second trimester came and I was finally out of the woods or so I thought. At 21 weeks of pregnancy I went in for my routine prenatal visit and sonogram and was told I was two centimeters dilated and had to be admitted to the hospital until I give birth because I was at increased risk for premature birth and fetal demise. I went from the clinic to a hospital bed and stayed there for the next fourteen weeks. I had no income coming in except for short-term disability which was a very small amount and we did not have any money saved so it was impossible to cover all the bills with my husband salary at the time. After fourteen weeks my son was born and after a few days I came home. The bills were mounting and so was the frustration and the disagreements. I was going through some postpartum depression at the time also and that made the situation ten times worse. To compound it all my step father who raised me passed away the day after my son was born and I had mixed feelings of grief, anger, and frustration especially because I just had a cesarean section and couldn't travel so I couldn't attend his funeral to pay my last respects he had done so much for me over the years and now that he was dead I couldn't even attend his funeral, it was rough. We were struggling to stay married, we argued constantly and couldn't see eye to eye on anything. After some weeks I went back to work but the damage had already been done. During the time I was hospitalized we had to use our credit cards to pay some of the bills so when I came home we were in debts that we couldn't afford to pay back in a timely manner; our debts were high and our credit score was in the dumps. I had just given birth to my first child and it should have been a happy moment but instead all the other things going on overshadowed that happiness that should have been present.

The weeks and months passed and my hope was that with time the situation would change and we would be back in a place where we could work on our differences and salvaging our marriage but it was quite the opposite. We fought all of the time and it got worst with time. It got to the point where we were living in the same house but did not speak to each other and even when we attempted to speak it would end in an argument we needed to separate because the marriage was causing us both our sanity. My ex husband move out the first time and went to Trinidad. During that time he took my son with him so that I could finish nursing school. It would be two years before he finally came back to the United States and we continued to work on salvaging our marriage. The first couple months were good but the hurts from the first separation lingered deep and after a few disagreements we were back to where we could no longer function together in a healthy marriage, our marriage was falling apart once again only this time it did not recover. Our marriage eventually came to an end after my son's death and the birth of my daughter. The most important lesson I learn from my first marriage and divorce is until you heal from your past and learn how to love yourself you will never be able to love anyone else. There is no statement more true than "hurt people, hurt people" if you are in pain and unhealed from your past traumas it is impossible for you to build and maintain healthy relationships with anyone. Don't bring past baggage into your present because it will negatively impact your future. I wish I understood then what it means to love yourself before trying to love others. For many years I hated myself, I was disgusted by the person I saw in the mirror. I had gaping wounds everywhere and all I was doing was putting band aids on them hoping that they don't bleed so much that it affected other people. I didn't have a clear understanding of who I was and where my life was going and as a result I found it difficult to cope with the every day stress of life and couldn't deal with the curve balls that life threw me on a daily basis. I was a shame to admit that my life was in shambles or acknowledge that I needed help to heal from my past. I thought I hid my feelings very well but I was figuratively naked and all my wounds were exposed for the world to see. I had to find healing, I had to come to a place where I could begin to love myself and be happy with the person I see in the mirror every day. I had to stop feeling like the world owed me love and understanding when I didn't love or understand myself. Divorce is a painful thing but many lessons can be learnt from going through it. Divorce doesn't necessarily happen because of the people involved being bad people many times it is much deeper than what is portrayed on the outside and the conceptions of people on the outside looking in. The arguments, disagreements and irreconcilable differences is often times a much deeper problem than what is displayed on the surface.

Divorce is a hard lesson but nevertheless it provides wisdom to those going through it. Those until death do us part vows does not always mean physical death as is understood by most people. If a marriage is emotionally, spiritually and mentally dead then in the best interest of the people involved it is time to go in different directions, you can beat a dead horse as much as you want but that doesn't mean you can breath new life into it. I am by no means saying that couples shouldn't fight for and take every step necessary to save their marriages, what I am saying is if you have tried everything and nothing has worked it is time to set each other free, why stay married and be miserable and unhappy? My family doesn't necessarily believe in divorces and me going through a divorce was the exception to the rule. Getting a divorce was frowned upon by many of my family members but I knew it was the right thing to do at the time because despite we both trying very hard to make it work we could not salvage our marriage. In life you have do what's right for you and your life even when those closest to you don't agree. Divorce is always looked upon in some cultures as a taboo especially when it is initiated by a female but there is nothing wrong with distancing yourself from a situation that you know deep down in your heart would never work. Two years ago a colleague of mine lost her husband suddenly, he died from a heart attack. They had been married for thirty plus years and had children and grandchildren. About six months after his death we went out for lunch one day and her husband came up during our conversation. She said to me that God must really have strong dislike for her because her marriage had been living hell for the first thirty years, she had to endure infidelity, physical and verbal abuse, her husband controlled the finances and every aspect of her life even to what clothing she wore and how she did her hair; she was very unhappy. She said the last two years before her husband passed was the best two years of her marriage, her husband changed for the better and she was finally starting to enjoy some happiness in her life and that was when God decided to take him. I asked her why she remained in an unhappy marriage for thirty plus years and she told me if she every brought up the "D" word to her family they would abandon her for life. She would be cast out of the family for bringing shame to them. In her culture the men rule the home and his orders governed everyone in the home including his wife. While I respect people's culture, thirty years is a long time to remain in a place of unhappiness and just existing in survival mode because you fear being frowned upon and cast out from your family circle. There is an old saying "you never know where the shoe is pinching while others are wearing it until you have to wear it yourself." It is easy for people looking on from the outside to cast judgement and force their opinions and beliefs on others but put some of those people in the very same situation and I can guarantee you they would make similar choices. Now, if existing in a dysfunctional environment work for and you are at peace with it, then by all means do what makes you happy, nobody should judge you based on your decision. All human beings are subjected to making mistakes and I am not here advocating for divorces based on mistakes, because none of us are perfect. If you and your spouse can work through your differences, get pass them and build a loving, caring and trusting marriage that is always the goal; and would be the ideal solutions to all marital problems but unfortunately not all marriages bounce back from certain situations and some marriages are doomed for failure from the beginning especially in situations where the purpose of the marriage was not because of love and happily ever after to begin with.

Chapter Five

My sonshine:
The son God blessed me with

In my early adult years, I was diagnosed with polycystic ovarian syndrome; it is a medical condition that is characterized by lack of ovulation and absent or sporadic menstrual cycles. My menstrual cycle would come at random times and was unpredictable. Getting pregnant for me was a very slim chance, since I was not ovulating on a regular basis. One morning I got up and had a queasy feeling to my stomach, I was feeling nauseous and felt like I was going to vomit. I was trying to trace back to all I had eaten the day before to figure out what was contributing to this feeling. I took some Pepto Bismol and headed out to work hoping that these feelings would soon pass, but it lingered throughout the day and never subsided. Several days passed and instead of going away the feelings got stronger and now I couldn't keep anything down. I was vomiting every time I ate or drank anything, I would vomit even after drinking a glass of water. This was not normal, there was something going on and I had to get to the bottom of it. I was working in the outpatient OB/GYN clinic at New York Presbyterian hospital at the time and decided to see one of the Gyn doctors in the practice. Because of my POS and absence of regular menstrual cycles my last menstrual cycles were three months prior. The first step was to rule out pregnancy since it had been several months since I had my menstruation. The pregnancy test came back positive, I was pregnant. At first I thought that somebody was playing a prank on me this can't be possible, I have POS and was told that I would need to get some type of medical fertility treatment in order to get pregnant, but now I am being told that I am pregnant. As the days and weeks went by I was becoming more sick from hyperemesis gravida and was in and out of the hospital for intravenous hydration due to my inability to tolerate any intake by mouth. In the first three months I had lost thirty three pounds and the fetus was in jeopardy, so I spent the first trimester in and out of the hospital. After the first trimester I started feeling better and could tolerate small portions of some foods so my weight started to stabilize. At week 22 I went for a sonagram and was told that my cervix was 2 centimeters dilated and I was at increased risk for preterm delivery. At that point my Ob/Gyn doctor decided to put me in the hospital until I give birth. I was in a hospital room that overlooked the Hudson river and I spent the next fourteen weeks counting the boats as they passed by on the water. My mother was at the hospital with me every day and would spend most the nights there as well. I couldn't get out of the bed or walk so the goal was to make sure I change my position every two hours so that I don't develop skin break down and stay in a reverse Trendelenburg position so I don't put pressure on my cervix and induce labor. At 26 weeks I started having contractions and was taken to labor and delivery because there was a strong possibility that I was going to have a premature baby if they couldn't stop the contractions.; fortunately after almost 24 hours the contractions stopped and I was back in my usual room.

It was the night of September 24th, and I had just finished eating dinner and was about to go to sleep when the contractions started, they were becoming stronger and more frequent by the minute and this time I was sent to labor and delivery but they were no coming back I was going to have a cesarean section and my son was going to be born. After signing consent and being prepped I was wheeled into the operating room for my cesarean section. It was about 1 AM in the morning of September 25th when my sonshine arrived into this world, kicking and screaming like he had been here before. He arrived at 36 weeks, four weeks before he was due to arrive but nevertheless he was here and I had finally met the child I was not sure would arrive after all the events of the last 14 weeks. My son was taken to the nursery and I was taken to the PACU to recover before being taken back to my room. Because of his early arrival and low birth weight my son was admitted to the NICU. After two days I was discharged home but my son remained in the NICU for another five days until he weighed five pounds then he was discharged home. This was my first rodeo with a new baby so I was still learning but thankfully my mother was there to help and guide me through the process. My son wouldn't nurse from the breast so we had to give him formula. There was a period of time when he would constantly cry and did not sleep at nights, my mother and I would be up with him most of the night trying to figure out what was wrong but couldn't figure it out. My son had a lot of gas and would cry and cry especially after he was fed. At one of his visits with the pediatrician I mentioned it and the pediatrician decided to have him tested for lactose intolerance, my son was allergic to lactose. The pediatrician changed his formula to a soy based formula and that did the trick; my son was pleasant didn't cry unless he was soiled or hungry and was sleeping through the night except to wake up once or twice for a bottle. My sonshine was growing and flourishing before I knew it he was two years old and running around the house.

After my son was born I realize that I needed to be financially stable so that I can take care of him and meet all his needs so I decided to go back to nursing school and pursue a nursing career so that I can increasing my earning power. I was working Monday through Friday 8 hours at New Presbyterian Hospital and going to nursing school on nights and weekends, my mom babysat while I went to work and school. My husband and I were going through marital problems and when my son was two years old my husband left the country and went to live in Trinidad and Tobago. It was becoming difficult to keep up with all the financial responsibilities in the home, so my mother went to work. At that time I couldn't afford a babysitter because I was paying all the bills in the home by myself. My husband decided that the best thing to do at that time was to send my son to Trinidad temporarily until I could get through school. Taking my son to Trinidad was hard, he slept with me every night, I was missing my cuddle buddy. During the time my son was in Trinidad I would travel back and forth every couple of months to visit and spend time with him, the days I was there was well spent but coming back to the US was always painful. Eventually I graduated nursing school and got my first nursing job at Long Island Jewish hospital a couple of months later my son and my husband came back to the United States that was one of the happiest times of my life. The family was back together and life was looking up, I was happy to have my son home.

After coming home I took my son to the pediatrician for a check up and to get him caught up with his immunizations. During the visit the pediatrician would ask my son questions and she noticed that he would repeat the questions instead of providing an answer, my son was displaying echolalia; this is a symptom that is prevalent in children with autism, so she referred my son for an autism evaluation. After all the tests were done my son was officially diagnosed with autism. When the official diagnosis was made I was disappointed but nevertheless I loved my son no matter what and we were going to get through this and make the best of it. The counselor got my son enrolled in special education and he was shining in his class. His teacher used to refer to him as her side kick. He was very proud of his work and would run up the steps every day after school to show myself and his grandmother what he had done in school that day. My son loved music and playing the guitar was his favorite thing to do. He loved reggae music and would sing the songs verbatim whenever it was played. My son was the light of my life, the reason I got up every day and did what I did he give me a purpose. His love was unconditional and without limits. He brighten every room he walked into with his contagious smile and his ability to sing in Spanish. He made me forget about all my troubles and give me a reason to keep going despite the barriers and challenges that presented themselves; he was my sonshine my ray of hope amongst all the turmoil of life, God had truly blessed me with a priceless gift. I had five precious years with my son, years that are forever etched into my memories. I remember with a smile on my face the day my son gave Elmo a bath and after the bath Elmo stopped talking and started screeching. He hated arguments and yelling and whenever there would be any arguments in the home he would starting shouting "guys, guys you are giving me a headache." Whenever one of us would celebrate a birthday he would serenade us with singing and pretending to play the guitar. He traveled all over the United States with his grandma, that was his favorite person outside of me and his father. Whenever he did something wrong he would run to his grandma before you could get to him. He was full of life and was a joy to be around. He was witty and the epiphany of "kids say the darnest things." Whenever his grandma would yell at him for one thing or the other he would say "grandma it seems to me that you are too bossy" he would just say the darnest things in the spur of the moment and we would just all laugh.

Chapter Six

"Oh death where is thy sting"
Living through death and grief

In 2007 my eldest brother was diagnosed with non-Hodgkin's lymphoma and his prognosis was poor. My mother took him to Trinidad for treatment but it was not successful so he returned home to live out his final days with his children. In May 2008, my brother passed away from complications related to his cancer at age 42. I was struggling to deal with his death but at the same time knew that all his pain was over and there would be no more pain. Flying home to Guyana to bury my brother was one of the most painful trips I ever took. Our family was grieving, my mother had lost a son, his children had lost their father and we had lost a sibling; we were all broken and trying to mend the broken pieces of our hearts. It was the first anniversary of my brother's death and we flew home to celebrate his life. After returning to the United States

I went back to work on the night shift at LIJ. It was just six weeks after returning from Guyana that death struck our family again but this time it was tragic.

It was Sunday, July 19th, 2009, I had worked the night shift Friday and Saturday and was sleeping so that I could go back to work on Sunday night. I got up that afternoon and went into the shower to get ready for work. I got into the shower and started showering not realizing that my husband had taken the bath towel to the laundry earlier that day and didn't replace it with another towel, so I didn't have a towel. I took my shower and was going to walk the short distance to my bedroom to grab a towel. I opened the bathroom door and was greeted with thick black and I could feel the heat on my skin. I couldn't go anywhere except towards the front door. I was naked but had no choice but to open the front door and exit outside. When I opened the front door there was a bunch of people standing outside on the sidewalk in front of the house. Some body came with a sheet and wrapped it around me as I was trying to decipher what was going on in the midst of all the confusion. I saw mommy with the baby in her hand some distance down the street but I didn't see my son, I was looking through the son but didn't see my son anywhere, I was asking where is Mekhi and somebody said the boy was still in the house. I started to run towards the front door to go back into the house but somebody held onto me and I vaguely remembered somebody putting a ladder to one of the windows at the side of the home in an attempt to try and get my son out. I was pacing back and forth with my two hands on my head when the firefighters arrived. The next thing I remembered was my son laying on the grass in front of the home and the firefighters performing CPR and then taking him away in the ambulance. I can't remember how I made it to the hospital but I was at the hospital. While at the hospital I was placed in a small room and told to wait for the doctor there. I started screaming and asking about my son, where he was and if I could go and be with him they said no you have to wait until the doctor sees you. The doctor came in a few minutes later and said "Mrs Fingal I am sorry to inform you that your son passed away, we tried to resuscitate him but it failed." I started screaming and tried to run out of the room but the doctor and nurses held onto me. I asked to see my son I wanted to see him and feel his pulse for myself. They took me to the room where my son was lying on a stretcher I felt his carotid artery there was no pulse, I felt his radial artery there was no pulse, I took my ear and put it to his heart there was no beat, I collapsed at the side of the stretcher and couldn't walk the nurses put me into a wheelchair and took into a grief room until somebody was able to get in contact with my husband and he arrived. The events of the next week are almost completely removed from my memory I was in a state of shock. In the days after my son's passing the rumor mill was rampantly turning, there were all kinds of conspiracy theories going around. Some even suggested that I had killed my son to get insurance money others that I had performed some kind of satanic sacrificial ritual with my son to get riches. The most hurtful part of it is that some of my relatives who had no idea what transpired on that dreadful day accused me of murder. I remember waiting for my husband in the grief room when three NYPD detectives came in and said "Mrs Fingal sorry for your loss, just want you to know that we will be coming by your now burnt home as well as asking questions of people in the neighborhood and whoever was in the home because of how your son died." I said ok please do whatever you have to do, I wasn't worried about their investigation because I knew I didn't have anything to do with my son's death; my only crime was working the night shift so that I could provide for my family and sleeping all day because I was extremely tired. I couldn't grieve for my son in peace, the pain I was feeling was indescribable; I had lost everything but most painful I had lost my son, whom I loved with every bone in my body. My son was on my life insurance policy and had a $10,000 dependent policy. The insurance company refused to pay for his funeral because they said they had to wait for the NYPD and their insurance analyzer to complete their investigations before they paid any money. I was grieving, already convicted of murder in the court of public opinion and there was a possibility that I wouldn't be able to have a decent and respectful funeral for my son because the life insurance company refused to pay. The pain was too much to bear, I could not sleep, eat, or think straight I had checked out, I spent my days drugged up on Xanax and even that couldn't take the pain away. My coworkers at LIJ stood in the gap for me and went to the employee assistant program director to get help. Three days after my son's death while my son's body lay in the morgue and I wondered what to do next one of my coworkers came to the relatives' house where I was staying at the time and handed me her cell phone it was the director of the EAP at LIJ and she said "Mrs. Fingal which funeral parlor is your son's body at and how much is the cost of his funeral?' I gave her the funeral parlor's contact information and she said she would call me back once she spoke to them. It would cost almost fifteen thousand dollars to give my son a decent burial, more than what the life insurance cost and it wouldn't matter anyway because they were refusing to pay. The EAP of LIJ agreed to pay for my son's funeral with the agreement that once I returned to work I would pay every month until I was finished paying. My son's funeral services and burial took place and I honestly can't say what transpired or anything about that day because I was there but not really there. I buried my son and walked away from Pinelawn feeling defeated, I would never see my first born again or hear him sing, or play the guitar which he loved. He would never again run up the stairs from school with his homework in hand or crawl into my bed at midnight to cuddle and sleep with me. I didn't know where I would go from here, I was walking back to the car saying "Lord why didn't you just take me?"

The months immediately after my son's death was hell. The pain of having to bury a child is enough to make a mother commit suicide, only those who have been through it will understand. I was going through a living hell. I was fighting through all the accusations of murder, from some of the people who should have been supporting me, life was rough but I had strangers, and friends who became family rallying and fighting with me. Every day was agonizing, I couldn't sleep, I had no appetite, I was rapidly losing weight and there was a constant indescribable pain in my chest. I was lost, helpless, hopeless, and angry at God, many days I begged God to let me die because I had no purpose in life, I constantly asked why he didn't let me be the one to die in that fire why it had to be an innocent child? I was drugged up on Xanax daily and was simply existing because I had stopped living. One day I was in so much pain I got up and told myself that today is the day I am going to take myself out of my misery. I picked up the bottle half full of Xanax and said I am just going to drink all of these pills and die at least it would be quick and painless. I went into the bathroom, locked the door, and opened the bottle with the Xanax in it, as I was bringing the bottle to my mouth my cell phone rang and the caller's ID said Long Island Jewish Hospital. I answered and it was the grief counselor from the EAP. She said, "Mrs Fingal I just want to call and talk with you this morning and find out how you are doing." I started crying and told her that I was having a rough morning but God had sent her. I never told her what I was getting ready to do when the phone rang, but the same God that is there for the saint is also there for the sinner; God didn't want me to go out like that. I took the remaining pills in the bottle flushed them down the toilet, sat there, and cried and cried, in the midst of all my pain God still had a purpose for me.

The house was burnt and we could no longer live there. In the first six months after my son's death we rented an apartment in Far Rockaway, about a block from Rockaway Beach; every day I would go to the beach and stay there for hours throwing rocks in the water, crying, talking to God about all my pains, asking him questions that I had no answer for I was in a very dark place. One morning I got up and was in severe pain and couldn't get out of bed, I couldn't walk or do anything for myself so I went to the emergency department. I was admitted and that is when I received my rheumatoid arthritis diagnosis. After being officially diagnosed with rheumatoid arthritis I spent the next six weeks in and out of the hospital because I had multiple flare-ups.

My marriage was on the rocks before my son's death and after he died it was officially over, my husband moved out and we went our separate ways, our marriage could not survive. We were bitter at each other and playing the blame game; in the end, it was best for us to go our separate ways and go through a divorce so that we could begin the healing process that was desperately needed at that time. The day the judge finalized the divorce it felt like I had experienced death all over again. I came home from court and was balled up in a fetal position for hours crying. In the last two years, I had buried my brother, and my son and now I was burying my marriage of the last ten years, physical and symbolic death was all around me and I was hurting. In the years that followed I lost myself, my self-esteem, and my self-worth, I didn't know who I was or what I was worth and my life choices were reflective of that. My choice of men where the poorest it had been in my entire life I was attracted to thugs and hoodlums, verbally and physically abusive men without vision or ambition; I was literally in the gutters. Death and grieve had me in a place where I didn't know who I was anymore. I knew I was in a dark place and I didn't want to be there and couldn't stay there but I couldn't find the strength to lift myself out. I thought the things I had gone through in life after leaving Guyana were bad, but nothing could prepare me for having to bury a child and the grief and heartbreak that would linger for years after; only the almighty knows how I survived those years. My days were long and dreary and my nights were restless and full of nightmares. I was literally living in hell on earth; my life was meaningless and without purpose. The sky was always gray and the sun seemed to have ceased shining; there was no rainy days every day was a storm. A good day for me would be the day I mustered up the strength to take a shower, comb my hair and eat a meal. Everybody was trying to tell me that I needed to let go and start living again, but nobody understood that grief is personal and everybody deals with grief differently. Grief and overcoming grief are personal and everybody deals with death in their own way. Some of the lectures I received on why I should stop grieving was harsh and selfish because the people giving those lectures had never had the experience of burying a child and could never understand how it felt. When a spouse die the surviving spouse is called a widow or widower, when a parent die the surviving children are called orphans but there is no name in the dictionary given to parents that lose children. If I was to give parents that lose children names it would empty, lost souls, with aching hearts that never heal. When I was younger a family friend of ours lost her only son in an accident. For years she cried and was going through major depression; everybody was casting judgement and saying that she was doing too much, I couldn't understand then what she was going through but now it is crystal clear. Death is inevitable and all of us will die one day but nobody is ever prepared to deal with death. Grief is an emotional and mental struggle that only those who feel it can describe and understand it. People see the outward display of grief the crying and unexpected outburst of sobbing but only the person grieving go through the psychological turmoil that comes with the grieving process. People can comfort a crying, sobbing person but only God can comfort the mind and soul of a grieving person.

Living in New York after my son's death was challenging and torturous. I cried every day for one reason or another. Whether it was passing the children's place, the school, the funeral home, or the school bus, it was a nightmare. After three months I went back to work feeling that it would be a distraction from all the turmoil of staying at home and trying to cope with grief. Going back to work was challenging. Every time there would be a cardiac arrest on the unit I would try to run the other way, I could not stand and watch or take part in CPR being done on anyone because all I envisioned was my son lying on the grass on the sidewalk in front of the house and the firefighters performing CPR on him. I would have nightmares almost every night, I could not control my thoughts, and they would constantly wander in all kinds of dark places. I was living in the what-if era. What if I didn't work the night shift, what if I did this and that differently, what if this and what if that, I was torturing myself. The nights were long and sleepless. The firefighters had given me a big blue teddy bear that they had brought from inside the burnt house. It was my son's teddy bear; I slept with that teddy bear next to me every night and when everybody went to bed, I would hug that teddy bear and the tears would freely flow. I would spend my days doubting God and his existence and would often ask myself the question if God is alive why would he allow such a thing to happen, especially to an innocent child? The burden of death and grief was wearing me down. I was missing my son and at the same time trying to be brave and strong for my daughter but everything around me was falling apart. I was trying hard every day to muster up the strength to get through that day and make it to another day; you never know how strong you are until you have to find the strength to carry on after you have buried a child. The big apple was starting to taste rotten and after almost twenty years I could no longer live in the city I once loved and called home, I had to leave New York City and again venture out to find a place to call home.

Chapter Seven

Rising from the ashes of the past

It was December 2011, and I was packed and leaving New York for Dallas, Texas. Leaving new York was bittersweet; while it was painful living there after my son's death, I felt like I was going away and leaving my son behind and that hurt. My son hated to see me cry and I know he would want me to be in a place where I am happy, and that brought me some comfort. Moving to Dallas, Texas was the first step in my journey to rising out of the ashes of death, pain, and unworthiness. I was determined to make my son proud, like look son your mama is making it despite all the cruel blows life has dealt her she is still standing, I know that is what my son would want; I was knocked down but not knocked out. In the ashes is a cold hard place to be but with God even the ashes can become a place to create a life story. God can take all the ashes of your past and mold you into a whole person again. "Yea though I walk through the valley of the shadow of death I will fear no evil for thou art with me thy rod and thy staff they comfort me" Psalms 23, verse 4 (The bible, NKJV.)

It was the end of December when we arrived in Dallas. In a few days, it would be January 2012 and I was starting work at Parkland hospital on the diabetes unit working the nightshift. I had my daughter stay in Guyana with my mother while I sorted myself out, I also was fearful of leaving her at home and going to work at night; it broughtback bad memories. I hoped that after a few months, I would get a dayshift position so that I could be home at night, and on the days that I was not working I would be able to take care of my daughter. I stayed with a family friend until I could find my apartment. I was meeting new people and making new friends. I have met some genuine friends while working at Parkland hospital and we remain close to this day. My daughter came home once I settled down, got my place, and felt comfortable navigating my way around Dallas. My daughter was my inspiration to strive to become a better person, she was watching me and I had to get it right. I was committed to spending quality time with my child, I know that tomorrow is not promised and I wanted to make sure that if something happened to me the memories I would leave my daughter would be good ones. We spent the weekends hanging out at traders village, ITZ, Hawaiian Falls, six flags, the movies, and any other place where we could spend quality time and have fun, we built a mother-daughter bond and it felt rewarding. In those days I was struggling financially and living from pay check to pay check and didn't have any money but spending the little money I had after I finished paying my bills to make my daughter happy was well worth it.

I transferred from the diabetes unit and went to work at Amelia's court in one of the outpatient clinics so that I could be at home at night with my daughter. On the days I went to work my daughter would have to be up by 5:30 AM so that she could be ready and dropped off at daycare so I would be on time for work. After work, I would be hurrying to make it to the daycare on time before they charge the $25 late fee and I would have a friend of mine pick her up and keep her at their home until I got off. By the time I picked my daughter up she would fall asleep in the car because it would be late. I was a single parent and life was rough, I was playing the role of both parents trying to stay positive against all odds for a child who was watching my every move. My daughter was struggling in school, she was sleeping in her classes and most of her grades were bad, as a parent I was failing my child. I felt guilty for all the early mornings she had to get up, the nights she was staying at other people's homes until I picked her up after work and the times, I was either sick or too tired and couldn't be there for her as I should. Life in Dallas was getting rough and my daughter was suffering as a result. I quit my job at Parkland and took an 8-4 job that paid less but allowed me to be there to drop my daughter off at school in the morning and pick her up in the afternoon. I put her into the after-school math and English program at Kumon, I would take her there every Monday and Wednesday and sit there for an hour while she completed the assigned assessments; after some months her grades started to improve. Kumon was expensive and having limited cash flow it was difficult but despite the financial constraints my daughter's education was worth it.

When I left New York I made a promise to myself that I would return every year at least one time to visit my son's grave. There were some years I couldn't afford to fly back and forth to New Yor to visit my son on his death anniversary or his birthday and I would be in severe physical and emotional pain when those dates came around and I wasn't there. I would be in severe physical pain from rheumatoid arthritis flare-ups and I would be in emotional pain because I felt like

I was abandoning my son. The times I did manage to buy us tickets to New York city we would stay in cheap hotels, you could smell the stench of mold and the aroma of marijuana down the hallways, the rooms were unkept and sometimes there would be roaches running around, but that's what I could afford at that time. Our trips would be no longer than two or three days in total. We would take the long Island to Pinelawn cemetery to visit my son, place our flowers, clean his grave site, hug, cry, and talk about all the little things he did which would result in laughter and break the ice in those sad moments, then we would take the railroad back down to Queens. The rest of the days would be spent visiting friends and relatives, walking down Jamaica avenue in Queens looking for cheap clothing and footwear, and window shopping, this was also the time my daughter would see and spend time with her dad.

I had no family or relatives in Dallas but over the years I developed and maintained close relationships with friends who became family. There was one Nigerian family that I met at my daughter's school and over the years we became family. The kids spent many weekends at our home and my daughter spent many weekends at their home. Their mother and I took turns picking the kids up from school and my daughter went to church, AWANA, and bible studies with them every week. My daughter loved her auntie Jennifer and enjoyed jollof rice and other Nigerian delicacies, she had a bonus family. I had found a sister in Jennifer and we developed a close bond. In addition, I had my childhood friend that I grew up with in Guyana living in Dallas and we continued to live and function like sisters, so my daughter had two aunties. I had two sister friends and our relationship was close and productive.

In April of 2016, my brother took a contract assignment at American Airlines in Fort Worth and would come by to visit. During one of those visits, he brought his wife and children and my daughter met her cousins for the first time. They bonded instantly it was like they had known each other for a long time. That summer she went on a month-long road trip with her uncle and cousins from Dallas to California, to New Orleans, to Indiana, and all the other states they stopped to spend the night in between, the girl went places and loved it. My daughter came home at the end of summer wanting to meet all her cousins and asking questions about the cousins she had never met, where they lived, their parents, and of course why she hadn't met them. That Christmas I took her to Jacksonville, Florida to my sister's house so she could meet her aunt and cousins. On the plane ride back home she couldn't stop talking about her cousins it was like she had found gold or some kind of precious stones, she wanted to maintain a relationship with them and was already asking when we were going back. When we got back home she was constantly bugging me about returning to spend time with her cousins and looking forward to next holiday season. Then one day she said mommy why don't you move close to uncle or auntie I have no siblings but at least I could have my cousins. At first, I dismissed it and told her I didn't want to leave Dallas I had settled there for some years and didn't want to start over in a new state again, but she kept nagging me about it. I thought long and hard about moving away from Dallas, Texas. I was trying to figure out what being close to her cousins would mean for us, where would we move that would be close to her cousins, I had two choices it would Indiana or Jacksonville, Florida. I didn't want to move back to a state where the winters were harsh and they had snow and if we moved to Indiana that would be our reality. The only choice left was to move to Jacksonville, Florida. The decision was made we were moving to Jacksonville. I started job hunting online, interviewed for and got hired at SHANDS hospital. My sister found me an apartment and in July of 2017 we left Dallas, Texas for Jacksonville in search of a new place to call home. At the time I was hired SHANDS only had a nightshift position available and promised that as soon as a dayshift position became available I would be given first preference to transfer. Several months past and every time I inquired about moving to the dayshift I was told there were no positions available. I did not want to continue working on the nightshift because it brought back bad memories so I took a position at Baptist on the neurology floor and left. Neurology was my first love so this felt like coming home. For the next year, I stayed at Baptist while I worked on my master's degree. I was still adjusting to life in Jacksonville and my daughter spent most of the time at my sister's house. There were some ups and downs during the time my daughter stayed at my sister's but she was in a safe place.

After being in Jacksonville for over a year I was still struggling financially so I decided to take a 13-week travel nursing assignment so that I could catch up on some of my bills. I spent the next thirteen weeks working in Tyler, Texas. During those thirteen weeks, I went to Chicago to attend the graduation commencement service for my master's degree and flew back and forth to Jacksonville several times on the weekend to visit. It was the night before Halloween and I had complete my final 3-11 PM shift and left Tyler for Jacksonville, I had promised my daughter that I would be home to take her trick or treating the next evening. It was around 7:30 AM the next morning, I was driving through Mississippi a few miles before crossing over into Alabama when I heard a huge noise, one of the tires on my car had blown out. I was on the highway in a remote town called Milledgeville, there were no buildings on either side of the highway only trees and clusters of bushes. The nearest tire shop was about ten miles off the highway and it took almost an hour for a tow truck to arrive and tow my car to the tire shop and then another two-plus hours waiting for the tire shop to purchase a new tire from a Walmart in another town since they didn't have any new tires in stock and since I had a long ride home they didn't want to chance it with a refurbished tire. I had no signal on my phone so my GPS wouldn't work while in Milledgeville, I had to get back on the highway using hand written directions from the tire shop owner, and by the time I crossed over into Alabama the sun had started to set, there was no way I was going to make it to Jacksonville to take my daughter trick or treating, I was disappointed. The next morning I was back in Jacksonville, Florida to resume my life. When I returned home from Tyler a lot had changed and my daughter no longer wanted to stay at my sister's home for many reasons. My daughter's behavior had also changed she was showing signs of anger and resentment towards me and I at first couldn't figure out what was going on but I knew I had to get to the bottom of it. One afternoon I picked my daughter up from school and I told her that we needed to have a conversation because I didn't understand what was going on. My daughter said mommy every day you were in Texas I heard that you left me and never sent any money to take care of me or bought me any clothing or shoes or didn't care anything about me. In addition, you never whooped me for eating food but I was getting whooped for eating food even if I wasn't the one who ate it, you need to stay here and take care of me. There was a lot said in my absence that I will not repeat in this book, but the entire experience was a lesson learned for me. The most important lesson I learned from my time living in Jacksonville is don't matter how you are struggling or how much hardship you are facing in life never leave your child at anybody's house or in the care of anyone else; keep your children with you and fight through your tough times. I came back to Jacksonville with my master's degree in hand and a job offer as an adjunct clinical instructor at Chamberlain University, my life started to change for the better. I started paying down my debts and I had extra money and was able to do things I couldn't do before. When I say the same God who is there for the saint is also there for the sinner I am living testimony he was turning it around for me. At the same time, I was trying my best to maintain a relationship with my family because if something happened to me that's probably where my daughter would have to go since I didn't know anyone else in Jacksonville. I was uncomfortable whenever I went over there because I was accused of stealing and didn't want to get that label put on me, the more I thought about everything that I heard I became more distant and knew that I had to distant myself it was time for me to protect my child and guard my peace of mind, there was too much going. I never stopped going to my family's resident but I did not go there as much as I used to in the past.

It was the day before Thanksgiving, 2018 and the entire family was on the road to Atlanta, Georgia to spend Thanksgiving at my dad's residence. On Thanksgiving day we cooked and ate and engaged in family chatter and friendly conversations. The next day was black Friday for all the wrong reasons it was a black Friday literally and figuratively. The events of that day made me realize that old feelings truly die hard or they don't die at all and continue to linger around after all these years. The next few days all the old anger and resentment I had from twenty-plus years resurfaced for several reasons, my anger was getting the best of me, and I was again in a place where I was letting my anger and emotions control me. I was acting out of character and can admit that some of my behavior was inexcusable. I was back to square one, in a place emotionally and mentally that I had fought very hard for the last twenty-plus years to overcome. I had to remove myself from this environment because it had just set me back some decades. The next two days I spent listening as everybody gave their opinions and cast their judgment. Sunday morning came and I took an uber went to the airport rented a car and left Atlanta with my daughter sitting in the passenger seat, something had to give, I had to find my way no matter what. During all the judgement and mudslinging back and forth on social media one distinct statement resonated with me "evolve or repeat". For many days I pondered on what that phrase meant to me. While I tried to put that phrase into context I also knew that there was no going back for me, I had to stand on my own two feet, I had to be one hundred percent responsible for my daughter and she had to stay at home. I had to stand up as a grown woman and weave my path. Monday morning came and I went to New Berlin Elementary School and changed my daughter's bus route so she could begin taking the bus to and from school from home. In the coming days I talked to my daughter all we had was each other and just as we did in Dallas, we had to make it work. I was working at Chamberlain and was in the first semester of my doctoral program. I would work 12-hour shifts three days a week and would leave the house at 5:30 AM and not return until 7 PM or later depending on the traffic on the 295. My daughter got home from school at 2:30 PM and would stay in the house until I arrived home from school; I would call periodically to check on her and remind her not to go outside or open the door for anyone. It was a scary period of time because my daughter was not at the age where she could legally stay at home alone, but thankfully nothing crazy happened. My days were long, after coming home from Chamberlain, I would stay up to complete discussion board questions, conduct research, and complete assignments. Most nights I wouldn't go to bed until 2 AM and would have to be up by 5 AM to be on the road by 5:30 AM. It was challenging but I was handling my business, paying my bills, and taking care of my child, all by myself and making it happen.

The struggles of single parenthood are many and you have to be a single parent to understand. My ex husband and I separated when my daughter was about 4 months old and got divorce when she was one year old. I obtain legal custody of my daughter and she has been living with me through her life. Her dad pays child support every month but I remain her main bread winner. It is difficult to have a social life when you have a child because you don't want to leave your child with any and everybody. I had to learn how to navigate work, school, and parenting. I had to be selective with my dating life because I didn't want to expose my child to men I couldn't trust so I rarely brought my child around people I was dating. After my daughter moved back home from my sister's house I knew that I had to go back to the days we lived in Dallas and had no family around, I had to readjust my life and routine to accommodate her and make sure she was taken care of. Some days were tougher than others and I had to step up during those extremely tough days and make sure my daughter knew that she was loved. Whenever they were donut days with dad at school my daughter would feel left out and inadequate because she didn't have a father or a father figure in her house that could go to school and represent her. It would be difficult for her during those times and while I tried my best to care for her I couldn't take the place of her father. Nevertheless, I was going to continue doing my best as her mother to ensure she knew she was my first priority. I didn't go to places she couldn't go and my life and activities was centered around her. My needs took a back seat because I had to cater to my daughter and her needs. I had to stand up for myself and my child, despite being only the two of us, we had to get through the tough days, which we did and our relationship became much stronger during those days. I started to gain my daughter's love again but most importantly I started to regain her trust, she was starting to understand that whatever I did was not out of abandonment but to make sure she was taken care of. The best way of apologizing for the days my daughter felt I didn't care was to show my daughter that the decisions I made were to make sure she was taken care even if they weren't the best decisions. I am human and imperfect but despite my shortcomings I want to be a parent that my daughter could look up to and be proud to say that I am her mother. Everyday I worked on rebuilding a productive relationship with my daughter, it was important that she did not grow up resenting me because she felt that I don't care about her or her well being. As a parent you never stop caring and loving your children and you always strive to do what is in their best interest.

Chapter Eight

"Evolve or repeat"
- what the phrase means to me

"Evolve or repeat," those famous words that was uttered to me during the family incident in Atlanta. For weeks I pondered on what evolve or repeat meant to and for me. Evolution is inevitable, it is an important necessity for our very existence and growth. Evolution takes many forms physical, emotional, spiritual, mental, and moral. In the context of the events that preceded that phrase being uttered, I was determined to put that phrase into prospective as it relates to my life. I was sitting in my classroom one morning getting ready to lecture on Maslow's hierarchy of needs and as I was sitting there I had that "aha" moment. Maslow talks about the need to feel loved, safe, and have a sense of belonging as the most basic human needs. Evolution is directly connected to being loved, feeling safe in your environment, and having a sense of belonging. Being loved is a basic desire of all human beings. What should being loved look like, is a question we all must ask ourselves. Love is patient, it is unselfish and kind, it does not boast, love is not painful and it does not hurt. When we tear others down because they see life through their eyes and not ours that is not love. When we slander, cast judgment and impatiently spread self-opinionated propaganda, that is not love. When we cause others pain and emotional harm with our words and actions that is not love. The most important element in love is self-love, if we can't look in the mirror and genuinely love what we see, how can we say we love others when we don't even love ourselves? The biggest hypocrisy in the proclamation of love is to be in church every Sunday shouting how much we love God but exiting the church doors carrying hatred for our fellow men. How does a person evolve in an environment where there is no love? More importantly, how do you heal in the same environment that wounded, broke, or damaged you? Does evolution mean sweeping all the hurt and pain under the rug, pretending it never happened and doesn't exist, and continuing to exist in an environment where you cannot grow and strive? Is living a lie worth it? Evolution for me meant turning a new chapter, learning how to love myself, searching my soul, letting go of malice, hatred, and judgment of others, and most importantly finding my place of peace. I had to learn how to forgive myself for all the times I cast judgment, practiced selfishness, hurt others with my words and judgment, all the times I engaged in idle gossip, and belittled others, most importantly I had to learn how to forgive others so that I can set my soul free from all the baggage that was weighing me down; forgiveness of self and others are important to evolution. I firmly believe that forgiveness and association are two different things. I can forgive but that doesn't mean that I have to associate. To evolve and not repeat I have to remove myself from anything and anyone that threatens to disturb my growth and my peace of mind and put me back into the dark place I once lived, I have to salvage that self-love

I have for myself and not go back to a place where I again start not feeling good about myself and who I am as a person. Painful experiences not healed from continue to hurt, "hurt people hurt people", there is no statement as accurate and true as this. To evolve and not repeat I have to take myself out of the environment that caused me pain so that I would not project my pains unto others. Safety is paramount to evolution. If you knew that if you ventured into a particular neighborhood at night there was a high probability that you would be robbed and killed would you still risk your life and go into that neighborhood at night? If you knew you couldn't swim would you go to the beach and go into deep waters without a life jacket knowing that you would drown? The answer to both of those questions would be no, the same concept applies to protecting the safety of our Peace of Mind as well as our emotional, psychological, and spiritual well-being. Cycles not broken become the norm and the norms eventually become cultures and are passed down from one generation to another. It is impossible to evolve in an environment where gossiping and judgment of others is a routine daily behavior. My daughter is watching my every move and learning from the lessons I am teaching, is this the type of human being I want to raise? Evolve or repeat, this phrase resonated time and time again. I had to end the cycle of generational curses that resulted in the reproduction of damaged men and women Who were simply replicating the norms of their ancestors. I had to pave a new path for my daughter who would one day be walking in my footsteps. Would I be the parent she looked up to or the one she can't wait to get away from? Would I be the parent that belittled, verbally, physically, and mentally abused her because that is how my ancestors disciplined and continued to walk in their shadows or would I go through a process of self-evolution so that so that I don't repeat their mistakes? Is it acceptable to create an environment where my daughter is fearful of me and she cannot be herself or tell me when things are going wrong? Or do I create an environment where she is nurtured, supported, and feels safe? "Evolve or repeat", when it comes to evolution I choose safety over cultural norms, ancestral trends, and generational curses.

As human beings, we all seek to be accepted and have a sense of belonging. Despite our differences, we want to feel accepted. There is none of us perfect, the only perfect man to walk the earth was Jesus Christ and even he was crucified by the same people that he broke bread with, healed, calmed their storms, rose from the dead, and turned their water into wine. Those were the same ones behind him denying him and shouting crucify him. The worst place you can find yourself is among hypocrites and Low key haters. You see them as friends and family and your feelings towards them are genuine but they see you as competition. They can have the whole world but still feel threatened by the little things you have accomplished. How do you evolve in an environment where you don't belong? Do you accept the status quo and continue to pretend that you belong so that you don't potentially hurt the feelings of those praying that you continue to walk in their shadow, hoping your star doesn't shine so it doesn't appear like it is dimming their light? Evolution begins the moment you realize that the only competition worthy in this world is self-competition, that unwavering commitment to strive every day to become a better person than you were the day before. To seek out find and walk in your divine purpose; to experience self-actualization, self-worth, and self-belonging. Evolution begins when you learn from the lessons life experiences have taught and heal from the wounds of your past so that you don't continue to bleed on yourself and others. "Evolve or repeat", is a phrase that needed to be planted in the subconscious of my mind so that I could explore its meaning on a personal level. It is the final day of the semester and the final day of nursing school for the seniors graduating. Today in my transition to professional nursing class I'm doing my final lecture on evolution, the importance of self-actualization, the understanding of love, safety, and belonging as outlined by Maslow, and how pertinent it is to evolution. Standing up, walking, and living your truth, is a basic necessity in the journey of evolution. Breaking barriers, societal trends, ancestral and cultural norms, so that the process of evolution can be a successful one. "Evolution", what a wonderful and fulfilling journey when you embark on it and not just preach it to others; there is power in words but even more power in actions. There is an African proverb that says, "if you escape from the lion's den, would you go back because you forgot your hat? (author unknown). "Evolve or repeat", go where you find love, safety, and belonging, embark on a journey to a place in your life where you can flourish, spread your wings, unequivocally be yourself, where you are accepted not tolerated, celebrated not envied, and most importantly where you find peace and Peace of Mind. When true evolution occurs you will be able to say like the Psalmist "it is well with my soul" and live it out in your life. My days of arguing and working through conflict with others are over, I will distance myself from anything and anyone that threatens my peace or peace of mind. I will remove myself from people or situations that can potentially put me back in a dark place so that I can continue to evolve and not repeat. People who hurt you will always try to manipulate others into focusing on how you reacted to the things they have done to you so that they can take the attention off of how they treated you that caused the reaction in the first place. Evolution has different meanings for everybody because everybody's journey is unique and different, we can't all set out on the same journey, each of our journeys will require us to take different paths; the more you understand where you want your journey to take you the less you are willing to compromise and accept things that do not align with that journey. Every day I continue on my journey of self evolution, it's a personal journey for me one that I must take on my own terms, it's a journey that only the almighty can take with me because he understands me better than anyone else in this world. As I continue on this journey I am grateful for all the fail ventures and set backs because they have taught me never to let your past define who you are, what you are capable of and where you are going. My past is behind me and I can't allow it to hinder my future, even if others are trying their best to resurrect my past to use it against me I can't look back, I have evolved. I can't let the death sentences cast on my future by people who are just waiting to hear the bad news of my failures deter me from self evolution, I have to continue to evolve in spite of. To never experience failure is to never try; failure is an integral part of evolution because it helps you to identify your weaknesses and at the same time build upon your strengths; it takes a strong person to continue evolving after they have experienced failures. Over the years as I continue on my journey to self evolution I learn to ignore the useless chatter of those who are still focused on my past and the failures of my yesterday because I realized that the only reason they are still focused on my past is because they have no access to my present life, they know the old me, and they can only discuss what they know. It amazes me when people continue to highlight and discuss things that I have done when I was 15 or 20 years old. I am almost 50 years old now, a person has to be really idle to still take time out to talk about things that occurred thirty plus years ago. That speaks volume as to who they are, obviously they still have refused to evolve and are still stuck in the yesteryear. I cannot help that they continue to be consumed by bitterness and self hatred that they feel the need to project their unhappiness unto others by continuing to highlight and focus on their past, I don't live there anymore and haven't lived there for decades. You shouldn't preach evolution to others if you yourself refuse to evolve; evolution is an action word and is evident by the things we do not the things we say.

Chapter Nine

Through a daughter's eyes

I grew up in a home where my mother and her husband even though separated continued to reside together. I was born during their separation to someone my mother was dating outside of the home. My biological father left Guyana for the United states when I was 8 years old. I was a little girl and vaguely knew who my biological father was, the little I knew of him was from photographs or as told by my grandparents, aunts, and uncles. I grew up with my step father and even carried his last name. My step father was cut from a different cloth and it was evident in his mannerisms. He treated me like his biological child and we had a strong father-daughter bond. He was my confidant and best friend, I had everything I needed and he was a great role model. Whenever things were going wrong in my life I would go to him, he would let me cry in his arms and assure me that everything would be alright

As a child I would anxiously sit at his bedside at night with my siblings to hear him tell Nancy stories and wouldn't move until he told the story of "Alibaba and the forty thieves" which was my favorite. After some years we moved from Savannah park housing scheme and went to Amsville Housing Scheme (41 scheme) but the relationship between us remained strong until I left the shores of Guyana for the United States. Two days after my son was born my step father died. I just had a c-section and couldn't go home to Guyana for his funeral, but I was hurt and in pain, I had lost a father and my son had lost a grandparent. I cried for a long time but I was also comforted by the fact that he lived his life showing love and compassion for the people around him, even me a step-child felt genuine love from him. My confidant and the best story teller in the history of my life was silent forever. I can't call him to pour out my soul and cry when life threw me lemons, he would never tell my favorite story ever again, I was heart broken. I still remember him on my birthday, his birthday, at Christmas time, or whenever I am going through my storms. He was the only person that let me cry and understood my tears other than God. He was always proud of me and made sure he told me that every opportunity he had, he always encouraged me to keep pushing despite my setbacks. A great man and beautiful soul has gone to his eternal resting place but his memories live on every day. Every time he flashes across my mind now I smile and say limp on limpy, limp on in heaven your time on earth was well spent. Your life on earth was a true reflection of unconditional love and the power of giving of yourself to others. God blessed me with you for several years and for that, I am forever grateful. I know you would be proud of me and everything I have achieved despite all my storms and troubled waters, rest assured that you have taught me well.

It was February 19th, 1996, I was 20 years old and leaving Guyana for the United States to live with my biological father. As mentioned before my father left Guyana for the United States of America when I was 8 years old. The next time I saw my father I was 17 years old and already teaching at Viola Nursery school. Throughout my childhood days, my father and I communicated through telephone conversations and the mail. Periodically my father would send money to my mother to assist financially but my mother and step father were the primary bread winners in the home. Because my father was in a different hemisphere we never truly formed a close bond as I didn't see him and didn't know him, but I always knew who my biological father was. Leaving for the United States was an opportunity to build a healthy, productive father-daughter relationship with my biological father but for many reasons that relationship never cultivated or flourished. At different times we both have tried to repair the broken pieces of our relationship and move on but it has never lasted. Many people have told their versions and given their reasons why there is a nonexistent relationship between me and my biological father and because I refuse to go back to the past I will not defend myself or try to convince anyone otherwise. I spend many nights talking to my almighty father about this situation, I have asked for forgiveness for whatever I have done to contribute to the situation and I am at peace with myself; I know my heavenly father knows my heart and because of that, I continue to trod on. I refuse to engage in pointless banter from people who want to come to me with judgment and rebuke for a situation that they don't know or have a full understanding of. If you are not coming to me with solutions don't attempt to bug me down with rhetoric and unnecessary problems. I am not interested in listening to hypocritical one-sided judgment from anybody. It takes a lot for a child and parent to get to a point where there is no relationship between them, only the almighty can fairly judge this situation so I am going to continue to leave it in his hands.

Every time I think of the role of a father I am reminded of the story of the prodigal son. The son went to his father and demanded his share, got it, and took off as the father watched helplessly in tears as he vanished out of sight and into the unknown. Despite his son's wrongdoings the father's love for him never wavered, he hoped and prayed every day that his son would come to his senses and return home. The father never lost hope and every day he was on his knees praying for his son. He didn't air his dirty laundry in public, he didn't disown him, he didn't put any stipulations on how he would have to act if he wanted to return home, he didn't sit down with his siblings and belittle him instead he looked for him everyday longing to catch a glimpse of his son walking through those gates. One day as he was looking he saw his son coming he ran towards him and welcomed him with open arms, it didn't matter where he had been or what he had done he was still his son and he loved him unconditionally. As parents, the goals should not be for our children to walk in our footsteps or do the things we have done and become us. The goal should be to support and empower our children to seek out, find, and pave their own paths with our guidance. They shouldn't be forced to look at life through our eyes but create their own vision. As parents, our love for our children should be unconditional and like the prodigal son whenever our children go astray we shouldn't belittle and disown them but embrace and encourage them, be their source of love and support not another battle they have to fight, our children are already subjected to all the elements of this cruel, evil world, the last battle a child wants to fight is with a parent.

When I was a child growing up I was always told that a child should be seen and not heard, they should do as they are told and never question an adult. Children were being raped, molested, physically, verbally and mentally abused, and had to suffer in silence because they were taught that it was disrespectful to question adult behaviors. Those children grow up angry and resentful and are shunned by the same people who told them to keep quiet. Teach your children that there is nothing wrong with speaking out against adult wrongdoings. Build strong, positive relationships with your children that are based on trust and honesty so they feel comfortable coming to you when something goes wrong. Listen to your children, do not try to silence them; not only listen to your children but let them know that you hear them and you understand. Your home should be a haven for your children the place they find peace when the world is against them. Speak positivity, life, and success into your children, support their dreams and aspirations, and always be there for them when they are at their lowest and in their most vulnerable state. Parents' love for their children should be unconditional and without stipulations; all children should be loved equally and no favoritism should be shown to any child. Parents don't always have to see eye to eye with their children or agree with their decisions. Parents must lead by example, our children are watching us and they are figuring out what type of parent we are, what type of husband, wife, sister, brother, relative, or friend we are, our values, and how we treat other people, especially people that can't do anything for us, but most importantly they are going to figure out how much effort you have and continue to put into them and their well being. Once they figure you out, you are either going to be someone they look up to and respect or someone they cannot wait to get away from and never want to be like.

Invest in your children and teach them the importance of investing in themselves. Teach your children how to pray and go to God when the cruelty of this world rears its ugly head, and you are not around. Show your children that you love and care about them and teach them how to love so that the love you give to them can be reciprocated. Be respectful to your children and they in turn will respect you, respect is earned not given. It's a child's job to respect and honor their parents but it is a parent's responsibility to give them something to respect and honor. Domestic violence is condemned, and the perpetrators are prosecuted and jailed for it yet some parents continue to physically and verbally abuse their children in the name of disciplining them with little or no repercussions. To spank a child is one thing but to physically cuff it out with your children leaving them bruised and battered with blackened eyes and swollen lips is abuse and should be labeled as such. When there is a problem in our relationships, marriages, partnerships, and situationships the expectation is that we reason it out and resolve it amicably but with it comes to our children it's "our way or the highway". I often hear parents say that children are not to be reasoned with, if they cannot follow the rules then they must face the consequences; consequences that include severe physical and mental abuse, refraining food and other necessities, and putting them out of the home with no foundation, unprepared for life on their own to face humiliation and disgrace. We are very impatient with our children, failing to realize that they are humans just like us and are subject to the same mistakes and imperfections as us. We treat our children poorly but expect that same child to love and respect us; we not only expect it but we demand it because we are their parents. Parents cannot break their children and hope that in the process of breaking them down, we somehow build them up, that's a cliché. We can't continue to ignorantly use the same parenting styles our fore parents used because that is how we have seen it done all our lives; you do what you know until you know better and when you know better you have to do better, ignorance is no excuse for continuing destructive and harmful behaviors.

After my divorce I was given full custody of my daughter and my ex-husband was given visitation rights. Once we moved from New York it was difficult for my daughter to continue developing a strong-bond with her dad due to the distance and financial constraints on both sides. The first few years after we moved my daughter hardly saw her dad and when she did see him it would be for a few hours.

As my daughter grew older I realized that she didn't have a relationship with her dad and even though she knew who her dad was there was no true relationship there. I am not the mother to discourage a relationship between my daughter and her father because we were divorced. I never had a relationship with my biological father and I did not want the same for my daughter; the father-daughter bond is a special one and every girl should be able to experience it. My ex-husband and I had to put our differences aside and find ways to get along because we are coparenting and our daughter's wellbeing is our number one priority. Over the years they have developed a strong bond and I love that for them. It is great to see my daughter experiencing something I never had the chance to, the cycle is broken and I am thankful for that. In addition, to having a father who supports and looks out for her my daughter has a great stepped-up dad in my husband who also supports and looks out for her so she is enjoying the best of both worlds; many days I wish I could take a look at the world through her eyes because it must be a great view: a view I would never have but the goal is always to give your children the opportunities you never had so I am satisfied.

For the children who have lost their fathers, don't know who their fathers are, or don't have relationships with their fathers, remember that you are valuable, you are worthy, and you deserve to be supported, celebrated, and loved just like any other child. Rest assured that your heavenly father loves you unconditionally and if you ever wonder away like the prodigal son just know that his arms are always open to welcome you back home. The same God that is there for the saint is also there for the sinner, he hates sin but unconditionally loves the sinner. I am a sinner constantly in need of grace, yet my heavenly father walks with me every day, he never leaves me or forsake me, and his grace and love are sufficient for me. Almighty father I know you love me despite my shortcomings and if the entire world writes me off I can find solace and peace in knowing that you will never leave me or forsake me and that is my reassurance every day that there is someone who loves me and is always there for me even in my darkest hour, as I am looking through a daughter's eyes.

Chapter Ten

Blood is not always thicker than water and definitely not thicker than peace of mind

Other than death nothing else bring people together like drama. People love drama and wherever there is drama people will gather. People will gang up against you just to keep drama going. In the weeks and months after the Thanksgiving 2018 Atlanta incident there was plenty of drama going on. There are people that I hadn't spoken to in years, who didn't even have my phone number or any kind of relationship with me getting involved in the drama. People were calling and messaging me on social media with all the tea and drama they were fed. Everyone had their version and spin on what had transpired and was giving their opinions accordingly. Family drama empowers everyone to get involved, if they are not putting their two cents in then the drama is lacking sweetness. I was out numbered, there was the entire family on one side and then there was me, the black sheep on the other side by myself, it was me against the world but I wasn't giving up or giving in, I had to stand my ground. All this drama was unfolding around me, family members were on social media posting their subliminal messages of attacks, sending all kinds of garbage to my inbox, calling me with all kinds of drama. At first I was angry and responding to all this nonsense, but after awhile I realize that I was entertaining these people and their drama and it was taking time away from the important and relevant things in my life. I had to come up with a plan to protect my peace and peace of mind. I got up one morning and I took a pen and paper and started writing my response on a notebook, I decided that I had to put all this drama to rest. After I had written my response, I opened my social media page and posted what I had written down so that all the people jumping into my inbox to chastise and cast judgement could all have my public response and this would be a good opportunity for them to speak publicly, all the things they were saying to me in private. Posting my response was the first step in killing this drama that was consuming my life and distracting me from the things I needed to do for myself and my child. All the pharisees lingering in my inbox to cast judgment not one of them publicly responded to my post, instead they took screenshots and sent them to all involved and even those not involved so that they could keep the drama going, I expected that. They were a few genuine family members that knew all that had transpired in the past and reached out in support and I respected them because it took strength to go against family. The entire family was against me and they were not going to stop until they had literally buried me alive, buried my character, buried my parenting skills and everything else they could find, it was assassination time and they were not going to let up until they had put the final nail in my coffin. I was not going to go down like a punk though I was going to fight back not by adding fuel to the drama but by isolating myself so that I could find peace. After posting my response, I set out on a path of self isolation. I went through my phone and deleted and blocked anybody that was contributing to this drama. The next step was to block and delete those same people from my social media platforms. After that I changed my phone number and even my name on social media, I was done. I was no longer going to entertain or be a part of any family drama. These people were determined to destroy me in any way that they could but in the process of destroying me they also was trying to destroy my mother and her character and that was the point when I said that is enough, assassinate me but leave my mother out of this drama. I had been burned repeatedly by family but this was going to be the last time. After my son's death, I took my then three years old daughter to California, I wanted her to meet my grandfather and her great grandfather because he was sick and I wanted her to meet him before he passed away. I was sitting in my sister's living room and a family member came over to visit, he said to my daughter "you are very lucky to be alive, you know your brother and the whole fire thing." My daughter being so young didn't understand what he was trying to say but I understood because the family was some of the main people spreading the theory of me murdering my son for insurance money. I was furious because my son was on my insurance as a dependent he had a ten thousand dollars life insurance policy, his funeral expenses cost way more than ten thousand dollars so what insurance money was I going to get from his death? The next time I went to California was when my grandfather died. I was at one of my uncle's home after the funeral concluded and one of my cousins said to me "what's up with that ugly hair style you have, that's really ugly." I never responded but I had decided there and then that I was not going around family any-more. There is this hatred that is very evident every time I was around family and they made sure I was aware of it by the things they would say. There is always a negative spin on my achievements, I wasn't capa-ble of achieving anything in life unless I was cheating to get it. I had to separate myself from family and family drama for the sake of my sanity and peace of mind. Family members have to understand that you cannot hurt people every time they come around and expect them to forget about it and keep coming around and associating because you are family. I am adamant about protecting my peace and blood is not thicker than peace of mind, if your actions have the potential to disturb my peace I am not associating with you in anyway, I have to prioritize my peace and my peace of mind.

As a child, I was taught that blood is thicker than water and you must always put family first no matter what. Family members built their foundation on that saying and it guided family relationships. It didn't matter how family members treated each other the expectation was that they forgive and forget because blood is thicker than water. I revered that statement throughout my childhood and into my adult life, but as I grew older my perception of this started to change. Some families are plagued with pedophilia, child molestation, rape, incest, verbal, physical, and mental abuse, yet those behaviors are swept under the rug, tolerated, and kept as family secrets all in the name of sticking together no matter what. Generational curses continue to hinder the success of future generations because some families refuse to confront the demons of the past. Their children and their children's children continue to suffer while parents and grandparents turn blind eyes to the wrongdoings of the ones who claim to love them and have their best interests at heart. Sometimes it is necessary to severe ties with the family you are from so that it does not destroy the family you create. You must figuratively wash and cleanse your blood so you don't pass down contaminated blood to your children. No one is more hated than the person who chooses to break generational curses and speak out against family oppression and wrongdoings. When family members feel comfortable saying that yes they speak derogatory about other family members but that shouldn't affect their relationship because every family does it there is a major problem. When did it become acceptable to degrade, belittle, and talk derogatory things about other people under the pretense that blood is thicker than water so they shouldn't be hurt or offended by it? Because blood is thicker than water when these things occur the expectations are that family members should see it as the norm and continue to stick together while their character is being assassinated, make it make sense. An old Guyanese saying, "When your own louse bites you, you are well bitten" (author unknown). When your own family set out on a mission to bring you down and assassinate your character only almighty God can save you. Family members are expert deep sea divers, when they are determined to bring you down they will go to the bottom of the sea to dig up your past sins from thirty, or forty years ago to make the case as to why you should be crucified. Whenever one parent abandons you, the entire side of that family also abandons you and they use every opportunity they can get to ensure that every member of the family develops hatred and resentment for you even if they have to feed them lies. They hate you but monitor your life closely and chastise any family member that dare to try having a relationship with you. They set out on a mission to hurt you to your core and bring you down; thankfully despite of their efforts I am still standing because the man that stand beside me is much greater and more powerful than those who stand up against me, his grace and mercy keeps me and propels me to higher ground, even when the odds are against me.

Family members are experts at keeping tabs on all your wrong doings; they can count with accuracy how many men or women you have had in your life, how many sins you have committed, the dog or cat you killed when you were five years old, how many times you cheated your way through school to get in the position you are currently in and any other thing they can add in their quest to bring you down. They find pleasure in passing judgment on others while they are piss-poor morally; as they are working diligently to expose the sins of others all the skeletons in their closets are spilling out. Some family dynamics are passed down from generation to generation because regardless of how destructive it is, this is how the family operated for centuries and nobody is willing to embrace change. To pave a different path for your children and their children you must stand up against destructive family traditions, break away from toxic and self-limiting family practices, and break longstanding generational curses. Breaking generational curses requires speaking out against child molestation, rape, and incest, confronting and addressing those dark family secrets and demons that continue to haunt your children and hamper their future, we must address the white elephant in the room. Blood is not thicker than peace of mind, you shouldn't have to turn a blind eye to wrongdoings in the name of family unity and sticking together while you compromise your peace. Sometimes you have to leave your family behind to pave a path of success for yourselves and your children. You have to choose to protect your children from things your parents and grandparents failed to protect you from so that you break the cycle of raising scarred, damaged men and women.

There is no question that family is important, but when family creates more harm than good, then there must be an evaluation of where you stand in your family's life and what roles family will play in your life. What are the benefits or consequences of continuing the relationship you currently have with your family members is it contributing to or stagnating your growth, is it bringing peace and peace of mind, or contaminating and destroying your soul? Family can either make or break you. You have to get to a point in your life where you tune out negative family judgment and don't allow them to bring you down. You have to realize that you can never please people especially family and focus on living your life the way you want to. This is your life and your story to live and tell, make the necessary edits that you have to, and never apologize for living your story in your best interest. Define and pave your path, and use the bricks from your past that are being thrown at you as stepping stones to build your foundation. Seek out and find your divine purpose, ask God for discernment and clarity. Everybody doesn't have your best interest at heart even some family members and you are going to have to drop off anything or anybody that weighs you down when you set out on your journey of walking in your purpose, or you would never reach your destination. Don't carry garbage with you on your life's journey, you can't eat it for nourishment if you become physically, mentally, or spiritually hungry, unless you are comfortable eating out of trash cans. It is acceptable when you identify unhealthy patterns in your family to break those patterns, so you don't pass them down to your children. It takes bravery to decide that unhealthy family patterns stop with you because you have to be prepared for the ridicule that will accompany that decision. You have to prepare yourself to be villainized, chastised, and cast out of the family, every effort will be made to break you and bring you down, but do not crumble, you are on the right side of history; continue to break down barriers of generational curses so you can set your children and their children free. You have to rid yourself of generational baggage to be successful in the future. Blood is not thicker than peace of mind, never accept the status quo in the name of family unity and sticking together; empower yourself to speak out against wrongdoings, and protect yourself and your children from harmful and destructive family norms and traditions.

Chapter Eleven

"To rest in peace or live in peace"

*E*very time I attend a funeral, the funeral home or church is always packed to capacity with people from far and near. People get up to give flamboyant speeches in memory of the dead. Family members who have not seen each other in decades take this opportunity to gather and ketch up. People at odds with each other take this time to find temporary peace and try to publicly get along for the sake of the strangers watching on. Foes become friends and enemies become frenemies in public displays of unity. People try very hard during this time to show they care and do everything in their power to convince the living that they had a good relationship with the decease. We promote love and togetherness and advocate for peace because life is short, and tomorrow is not promised to any of us. On the days during the planning of the funeral we write poems and sign songs, and all our intentions seem pure and unselfish. We embrace each other with hugs and kisses and shower each other with kind words and sentiments. During those days selective amnesia step in and we conveniently forget all the ill will we have imposed on each other before death came knocking at our doors.

Every day new babies are born and as they make their entrance into the world people both young and old are dying and making their exit from this world. Every day our social media timeline is flooded with announcements of death, condolences and rest in peace posts. When our loved ones are alive we slander spread hate, belittle, and demean them, but as soon as they die we look through our photo gallery and resurrect photos and videos of happy times and post them on social media with long paragraphs depicting beautiful memories and messages of love; we paint this perfect picture of them, cry crocodile tears and post subliminal messages of" return if possible" and" I wish heaven had a phone." We hypocritically get up at their funeral service and eulogize them in a way that would make even a stranger listening shed tears. We embark on a charade of public display of grief and tear our garments to show the world that we care. We post memes with wishes that heaven had a phone meanwhile when that person was alive we never picked up the telephone and called them. We shower the dead with expensive wreaths and bouquets but when they're alive we don't even care enough to buy them a single rose. We assemble beautiful collages and display them on big-screen television to paint a perfect picture for the world to see. We forget about all the pain, ill-treatment, discrimination, mental and psychological anguish, lies, and hurt that people experience while they are alive because of us. We forget about all the years we assassinated their character and didn't care about their well-being. Nothing brings people together like death. People will fly long distances to come and bury you when you die but wouldn't lift a finger to pick up the phone when you are alive to call and check up on you. It's easier to type RIP when someone dies than it is to live in peace with them when they are alive. My motto is "If you don't care about me when I am alive save yourself the drama and expense and don't come and pretend when I am dead. Don't come and use my death as a masquerade to get attention, or fool people into thinking that you cared. Let the people who genuinely cared and gave me my flowers while I was alive be given their space to grieve and celebrate my life. If you didn't love or care about me when I was alive it would be impossible for you to suddenly love and care for me when I am dead and can't feel or appreciate it.

We are more comfortable typing RIP than we are living in peace. There would be an entire church or funeral home filled with people coming to get one final glimpse of your cold lifeless body but most of those people haven't seen you in decades while you were alive. It is easier to celebrate your life after you die than it is for people to celebrate with you while you are alive and can acknowledge and appreciate it. It is easier for people to stand at the side of a casket and profess their love for you when you cannot hear than it is to show you love when you are alive and can feel it. It is easier to be carried by six when you are dead than to be uplifted and carried by those who claim to love you when you are down on your knees and struggling through hardships when you are alive. It is easier for people to cry over your body when you are dead than it is to hug and cry with you when you are in mental and emotional pain. Most of the people crying over your dead body and showing public displays of grief and anguish did not take any of the opportunities they had to show they cared while you were alive. We are living in sad times where people go out of their way to sympathize in times of death but have no empathy for the plight of their fellow men while they are alive. The only certain thing in this world of uncertainty is death. Death is inevitable and we all will die. Tomorrow is not promised to any of us, we are here this minute and gone the next, yet we consume ourselves with greed, hate, grudges, selfishness, and pride and fail to spread love in this cold, cruel world that desperately needs it. Why just rest in peace why not live in peace, the dead cannot feel or appreciate love, so why not live in love not just attempt to demonstrate love when it cannot be felt or appreciated?

The more we understand how short life is, the more we strive to live in peace; we are more inclined to give people their flowers while they are alive and not waste money showering them with flowers when they are dead and have no knowledge. The goal in life should be to cultivate loving, caring relationships with the people in our lives so that when the time comes to write RIP and show our final respect to the dead it is genuine. Death should be a lesson to us to change the way we live, but many of us use death as an opportunity to convince the living that we care about the dead. After the funeral services are over we return to our homes and continue our daily routine; back to gossiping, backbiting, selfishness, and all the toxic behaviors we engaged in before. We don't stop to think that life is short and tomorrow or even today could be the day to die, if your number is called tomorrow what kind of legacy you are leaving behind? When we die the only legacy we leave behind is the memories we created while we were alive, what would be people's lasting memories of us; would they be good memories or memories they wish to forget, did we live in peace or the goal was just to die and hopefully rest in peace?!

Chapter Twelve

Finding peace in isolation: choose you

It is not selfish to vibe alone for a while to find yourself. Distance and silence are the best tools you can use when you embark on a journey of self-discovery. When there are a lot of distractions in your life it is difficult to ignore who they are telling you to be and learn who you are. Because everyone cannot go on your journey with you some chapters in your life will have to be closed. You have to find your calm era, stay focused on your journey, and walk in your purpose. When you are in your calm era you refuse to deal with any negativity, drama, confusion, or conflict and you have to isolate yourself from anything and anyone creating it. It doesn't make sense to engage in or give energy to anything or anyone trying to disrupt or destroy your peace. Distance yourself, walk away, ignore, block, delete, and eliminate anything that compromises your peace of mind. Get rid of all monitoring, and destructive spirits in all its forms, and sometimes to do that you have to isolate yourself from certain things and people. Value the times spent in quiet places by yourself, it allows you to think, problem solve, and come up with solutions; it allows you to recognize what your needs are, where you want to be, and how you are going to get there. During your time in isolation, you can openly speak to God, ask for direction, and communicate with your inner self. Isolation puts you in tune with God and yourself; it takes you away from all the noise and distractions of the world and helps you to find clarity in your thoughts.

Isolation means setting boundaries, severing ties, and changing unhealthy and toxic behaviors. Isolation allows you to let go of things in your life that are weighing you down; it creates a distance that facilitates growth in all of its forms. To isolate doesn't mean to hate or despise anything or anyone, it prevents you from entertaining anything that is destructive and undermines your peace. It is not selfish to choose yourself. It takes tremendous strength to prioritize your peace and isolate yourself from things that will prevent you from experiencing true happiness. There is nothing wrong with choosing people who are beneficial to your growth and letting go of everyone else. When you make yourself a priority and spend time focusing on yourself there is no time left in your life for idle gossiping, fighting, arguing, being petty, or engaging in nonproductive conversations and dead-end situations. When you choose yourself and your peace of mind you become stingy with your time and what you invest it in; you can always recover wasted money but you can never recover wasted time. Beware of monitoring spirits, people who only show up when you are down on your knees and at your lowest and most vulnerable time in your life not to help but to monitor all your movements so that they can make sure to do everything in their power to keep you down; they provide a problem for every solution, they are not your helper, they are monitoring spirits. Isolate yourself from monitoring spirits their only job is to disrupt and destroy your peace, they closely monitor you hoping and praying that one day you fall and never get back up so that they can celebrate your downfall.

Isolate yourself so that you can experience true growth and flourish. Never allow anyone to use your past against you, we all have done things in our past that we are not proud of. We are born in sin and shape in iniquity, which means we are sinful and constantly in need of God's grace. I am reminded of the story of the woman who was brought to Jesus while he was teaching in the temple. The Pharisees came to Jesus and brought a woman who was caught in adultery and according to Jewish law, she was supposed to be condemned and stoned to death. The Jews were loudly chastising and condemning her and asking for her to be stoned for her sins, but as they were shouting, hurling insults at her, and demanding she be stoned to death, Jesus stooped down and wrote in the sand, "he who is without sin cast the first stone." There was complete silence, all the shouting suddenly stopped, and the only sound that could be heard was stones dropping and people walking away. When everyone had left Jesus was the only one still there with the woman, he told her to go and sin no more, if your accusers cannot condemn you, neither will I. She was standing there with the only man that has never sinned, yet he did not condemn her even though he was the only person worthy of doing so. Never be ashamed of your past, those were life lessons, not death sentences. Despite how many times people put you down or write you off, despite how many poor choices you have made in your life, despite your sins and shortcomings, find your peace and walk unapologetically in. People are going to talk about you whether you do good or bad, people are going to bring you before judgment halls and attempt to stone and crucify your character but remember that there is only one person qualified to pass judgment, he is the only one that sits high enough to look down on anyone. Every day you wake up decide to choose yourself and isolate yourself from anything that compromises that decision. Isolating yourself to find your peace will come with many challenges, but don't get discouraged and never quit. Isolation will require navigating through troubled waters and unchartered territories, paving your path, breaking away from the status quo, embracing your shortcomings, and learning from your setbacks. Be your authentic self because God can only work with the authentic you, he cannot do anything with the person you pretend to be.

Choose yourself unequivocally, and stop defending and explaining yourself and the decisions you have made in your life. Focus on your growth and choose your battles wisely. Don't be tempted to stop and throw stones at every barking dog you encounter on your journey, otherwise you will never reach your destination. You don't have to show up to every conflict that you are invited to, sometimes we take on battles that are not meant for us to fight and they drain, frustrate, and cause us to lose focus on our goals; know when to fight and when to walk away. Vibrate higher, find the right crowd, and let your voice be heard for the right reasons. Choose your company wisely, show me your company and I will tell you who you are. If the people around you do not add to your growth you are in the wrong company. Everybody is not your assignment study their content before you invest your time in them. In life one of our greatest desire is to be understood, but we have to get to the place where our greatest intention is to understand ourselves. When you understand yourself, it becomes impossible for others to manipulate you into accepting their understanding of you. To choose you, you have to stop doubting who you are and your potential. Don't sabotage your progress by doubting yourself and your capabilities. You have to believe that you are capable of and can achieve anything you set your mind to do and become anything you aspire to become. Doubt hinders progress much more than obstacles do. Doubt kills dreams and causes stagnation in growth.

Choose you and let your light shine. Don't dim your light because it is affecting unhealed, jealous people. You have to get to a point in your life where you decide what kind of life you want and once you make that decision reject anything that doesn't align with that decision. Your light is going to cause many people to hate you, shine anyway. Success is a journey not a race, and each chapter in that journey may require a little more; a little more thought, a little more effort, a little more self-assessment, a little more time, a little more patience, a little confidence, a little more faith, a little more strength, and little more endurance. Whatever we set out to achieve in life it is always going to require a little more. Learn from your life experiences and grow from them. Too many times we continue to focus on the pain and we don't emphasize the lesson we should have learned from that pain. Mistakes not corrected continue to be made, lessons not learned continue to be taught and painful experiences not healed from continue to hurt. To heal you must address those unhealed wounds, correct those mistakes that continue to throw a monkey wrench in your growth; learn from the lessons life has taught, and most importantly live in the here and now. Live your life to please God, not your fellow men; it doesn't matter what you do there is always going to be somebody criticizing you. Your life is your story and you are the author of your own story, don't waste precious time seeking validation from other people. Sometimes hate lives close to home it is ok to leave home if home is preventing you from growing and succeeding. Sometimes we have to venture out of our comfort zone to find our true home; not that place we continue to settle in just so we can say we have a home, but our place of peace. Become your biggest supporter, celebrate your milestones, clap for yourself, grow and glow, and don't allow anyone to steal your joy or downplay your achievements. After fighting so hard to get back on your feet after your numerous falls don't allow anything or anyone to knock you back down, stand up and stand firm.

As I am writing this chapter today the nation is celebrating Martin Luther King Jr, his fight for freedom and equality, his struggle to free his people from physical and mental slavery, his quest for Utopia, and his resilience in the face of imminent death. He was fearless, determined, had a vision, and was steadfast in his beliefs; he not only talked the talk, but he walked the walk. Change doesn't come without sacrifice, freedom doesn't come without a fight, and success doesn't come without determination and resilience. You cannot lead without vision and most importantly you cannot win when you are fearful. We are born to shine, there is greatness in all of us, but we have to get rid of fear and tap into our inner strengths. Fight for what is right for you and your life, be fearless in your quest for self-discovery, walk, stand up, and live your truth. Every morning you wake up and are blessed to see another day, unapologetically choose you. Choose to be happy, choose to love and be loved, choose to make a difference in a world that desperately needs it; choose to let your light shine. Self-love, self-respect, self-actualization, there is a reason they all begin with self because only you can attain them. Don't ever dim your light to fit in where you don't belong, and never compromise your happiness to make someone else happy; choose to be happy and do what makes you happy. Pack your bags and move to that new city or state, get that degree, buy that house, start that new business, go on those vacations, buy that dream car, take risks, and never regret anything in this life; if it didn't bring you what you want it enlightened you to what you don't want.

Chapter Thirteen

In the midst of it all

To survive in this world you have to be mentally, emotionally and physically strong and never give up no matter what you are going through. Tomorrow is a new day and the sun will shine again. The story of my life is filled with failures, disappointments, poor choices, heartbreak, depression, and death. Unfortunately, my life is familiar to many people because they have fought or have had to fight similar battles in their lives. In the days when you are on the brink of giving up pray through your hard times and continue pushing. For years I struggled silently with depression and don't be fooled depression is real. Every morning it was a struggle to get out of bed. Doing routine things was burdensome; bathing, putting on clothes, doing my hair, getting into my car, and going to work were all daunting tasks for me. Finding the motivation to do and enjoy the simple things in life was challenging. My moods were unpredictable, one day I would be happy the next day I would be extremely sad. Some days I felt like I had purpose and wanted to live and other days I was begging God to take me out of this world because I had no purpose. Some nights I slept through the night and other nights I would be wide awake staring at the ceiling impatiently waiting for the sun to rise. Sometimes I wouldn't sleep for several nights in a row and would be anxious, jittery and irritable during the day. I would get angry and be miserable for no apparent reason; I was living with depression. I would go several days without answering phone calls or replying to text messages, I didn't want to be bothered because I felt like nobody cared. I felt unloved, unwanted, and worthless. I was in survival mode; doing the bare minimum to keep going but not living; alive physically but dead, emotionally, mentally, and spiritually. I would attend church occasionally but was too tired and spiritually drained to grasp and apply the word to my life. I was living an unhealthy life; my sleeping and eating habits were poor and my mood fluctuated up and down, I was struggling to find balance in my life. My thoughts and actions were unhealthy and everything I did was detrimental to me.

It was Christmas morning 2018, my daughter had left for Connecticut to spend the holidays with her dad and I was home alone. I was lying in bed, scrolling through social media and someone had posted excerpts from a sermon by a reverend entitled "The Greatest Love". The reverend was breaking down Jesus' ultimate love for us and talking about loving ourselves and our fellow men. But there was one particular statement from his sermon that resonated with me, he said "many times we sabotage our happiness and fail to find peace because we look for love in everything and everybody else except the two true sources of real love, Jesus Christ and ourselves. We search this hateful world from corner to corner looking for something that doesn't exist but don't take the time to search and find the love that exists within us." I got out of bed, walked to the bathroom, and stood in front of the mirror and I said to myself "today is the last day, you let depression rule your life." I wanted everyone else to love me and seek validation from everyone else but I hated what I saw in the mirror; I didn't know my worth and couldn't figure out what my true value was. As I stood in front of the mirror I was tempted to crawl back into bed and consume myself with self-pity and the usual why me questions but the words from that sermon continued playing in my thoughts. I couldn't go back to bed; I took a shower, got dressed, got into my car, and left the house. I went on a joy ride to JAX beach, parked my car, took my boots off, rolled up my jeans started walking along the edge of the water, and started having a conversation with Jesus. Thankfully it was winter so the beach was empty otherwise people would have thought that I was insane and having a conversation with myself. I was having a full-fledged conversation out loud with the almighty. I said "Lord, I haven't done right or lived right, I am a sinner in need of your grace, I know you said come as you are but honestly it has been hard because I don't even know who I am, but today I want to change that, so this minute I am coming to you as I am. I know that you know who I am and I also know that you love me just as I am, help me discover who I am so that I can become who you want me to be." That moment was the turning point in my life, it was the day I embarked on my journey of self-discovery. All these years I was wandering here, there, and everywhere, from house to house, from state to state, from city to city, depressed and bewildered desperately in need of a place to call home, I had wandered far away from home, I was living in a strange land but that day was the beginning of my journey to find that place to call home. Home, my happy place where I could walk in the wellness of mind, body, and spirit. I walked back to my car, opened the door sat in the driver's seat, and started singing "When peace like a river attended my soul, when sorrows like sea billows roll, whatever my lot thou has taught me to say it is well, it is well with my soul." Many people in my position have either committed suicide or have spent time in a psychiatric unit of a hospital somewhere, but in the midst of it all God kept me alive and in a sound mind. Even in my unfaithfulness, disobedience, and rebellion the almighty not only kept me but put me in a place to make it right. As I was driving back to the house I said " Lord I don't know what your plans are or what you are doing in this season, but whatever it is don't do it without me, wherever you lead Lord I will follow. That night before I went to sleep I prayed for discernment and renewal of thought. When I opened my eyes again it was 6 Am the next morning I had slept through the entire night. This was the first day of navigating my new path on my journey home to self-discovery and self-healing. There is no greater reward than connecting to Jesus on a personal level; when that connection is genuine you truly become a new creature. You begin to walk in the newness of life, and everything about you changes; the people you allow in your life and space change, things you allowed and settled for change, and the men or women you used to attract and tolerate no longer mean anything to you, your habit of procrastination change, your spiritual laziness disappear. The self-hate you once had disappear, the things you used to do and the places you used to go that were destructive to your growth and inner peace become things of the past. My journey was personal I was determined to overcome depression and everything else in my life that prevented me from walking in the newness of life and finding myself.

One week later on a bright and sunny Monday morning, I walked into Chamberlain University to begin the new semester a changed woman. I was not where I wanted to be but I was not stuck in the same place I was a year or couple of days ago, I was moving out of my comfort zone and exploring my possibilities; I was a work in progress and there were many challenges along the way, but every time I slipped and fell, I prayed, got up, dust myself off and kept going I was determined not to go back. It was forward ever, backward never for me at that point the only time I was going to look back was to see how far I had come. When all else fails and people count you out, trust and hold onto Jesus he will keep you in the midst of it all and bring you through it all triumphantly, just as he parted the Red Sea so that the children of Israel could make their way out of Egypt to the promised land, he will make a way for you. When your pharaohs keep rearing their ugly heads and you can feel them breathing down your neck and all you can see in front of you is the roaring red sea and you can't swim and you feel that you are about to either be consumed by your enemies or drown in your sea of troubled waters, lift up your head because it is in those moments that the only person to ever walk on water will part the red sea and provide a path to victory for you.

Chapter Fourteen

Vibrate Higher, your happiness begins with you

After I had resolved in my mind that I wasn't going to let anything prevent me from being happy my entire prospective on life changed. I knew that the only person responsible for my happiness was me and I was not going to entertain anything or anyone who could potentially compromise my happiness; my happiness was my first priority. In order to be physically, mentally and emotionally happy I had to be mindful of what I fed my body and mind because we are what we eat. I wouldn't go to the store buy a bottle of poison and drink a small portion of it everyday knowing that it would eventually kill me, unless my intentions is to commit suicide. I had to apply the same principle to my emotional and mental health. I had to be selective in what I fed into my soul. If I surround myself with negative people and consistently feed negativity into my soul all my thoughts and actions would be negative. In the basic rule of gravity two negative cannot attract but in life this is quite opposite the more negativity we feed into our souls the more negativity we attract. Negativity does not promote growth rather it impends and is detrimental to growth. All my life I was searching for happiness and validation from others but this entire time my happiness was my responsibility and I was neglecting to look inside myself to find out. Happiness is a personal choice and nobody can make you happy unless you are first happy with yourself. Many people struggle on a daily basis to find happiness within themselves and people can only share happiness with others to the level of their happiness with themselves, so if there is no happiness with themselves there is no happiness to share with others. When you are truly happy with yourself you start to vibrate higher, your mannerisms and outlook on life change. You are selective with the things and people you align yourself with. My circle is very small by choice; if the people around me cannot contribute to or inspire me to grow I don't need them around, they have to go. I no longer sit at tables where they discuss other people, it is distracting, destructive and doesn't add any value to my life, it is wasted time that I can never recover. If they are assassinating other people's characters in your presence when you leave your character will be the next one on the table for feasting. When you start to vibrate higher you are going to lose some people that was once close to you, but don't look at it as a disappointment, count it as a blessing the rotten apples have to fall to make way for you to meet the people who you can grow with. Sometimes we have to move away from the known and into the unknown to receive the blessings God has in store for us. The Israelites had to leave Egypt in order to get to the promised land. They had to come out of their comfort zone and trust God to take them to a place of a higher calling; a place where he could fulfill his purpose in their lives. Egypt was not their home, in fact it was the opposite of the home God intended for them. They were in physical, emotional and psychological captivity. They had become complacent and were comfortable cohabitating with the enemy, they were living in the shadows of the Egyptians and had lost their sense of identity, they no longer knew who they were and started to adapt to the ways of their enemies because they thought that they had to fit in in order to survive. They were going to bed with the enemy hoping to wake up and their foes become their friends, but nothing changed. They consistently did the same thing but woke up every morning hoping for different results. The first step in evolving and vibrating higher is to assess your environment to determine if the people around you are with you or against you, are they your friends or your foes are they contributing to your growth or aiding in your stagnation, is this the place God want you to be or are you settling for the status quo? Are their conversations healing or creating wounds, are they healthy for your mind and soul, are they bearing good fruits or rotten apples that the worms eat? Are these people feeding your soul with good food or slowly poisoning it? When you start to vibrate higher these are legitimate questions that you have to ask yourself. If you consistently keep garbage piled up around you then eventually your value will also decrease drastically, you are a product of your environment. The children of Israel were doomed while they lived in Egypt, God had to take them out of Egypt in order to save them.

Sometimes in order to vibrate higher you have to change the people around you, you have to be very selective with the people and things you give your attention to and you have to make the hard choice to remove yourself from people and environment that no longer contribute to your growth. When I sit down with the people in my circle we discuss business and entrepreneurial opportunities, investing in the stock market, building generational wealth, empowering ourselves and each other. We discuss ways to ensure our children's future are secure that so that if anything was to happen to us they are not burdened financially. Show me your company and I will tell you who you are; the people around us can either make us or break us. It is more valuable to have four quarters than one hundred pennies. It is more beneficial to have a few genuine people around you that speaks positivity into your life and contribute to your growth than to have your space filled with empty vessels, unhealthy and unproductive banter. Learn the difference between your associates and your friends. Your associates are people you interact with on a daily basis out of necessity, your friends ride with and for you everyday and are there for you when your back is against the wall. Your friends are the people you can pick up the phone and call at any time and you know that they got your back. It's the people you can trust when you are down on your knees and at the lowest points in your life to cover you under their wings and not broadcast your downfalls to the world in your absence. You cannot maintain healthy and productive friendships with people not going in the same direction as you, your friends should inspire you to become a better person, they should add to your growth and help you to level up, not have you engaging in idle gossip and waddling in mediocrity. The people you have in your space will either make you or break you, choose your friends wisely, vibrate higher.

It is Tuesday, January 2nd, 2024 and I just returned from Guyana a few days ago. I am now settling back into my daily routine. My phone ring it is one of my sister friend. There is a delegation of women entrepreneurs going to Guyana for a women in business summit, she isn't Guyanaese and this is her first trip to Guyana. Today, we are networking, I am linking her up with people in Guyana that can assist her to navigate through different investment opportunities in Guyana. In addition, we are discussing other potential business opportunities in other places and collaborating with other women to highlight various entrepreneurial ventures in the states we currently live in. The conversation at this table is a productive one, the discussion is focused on money making ventures and women empowerment in business. We are focused on paving the way for our children so that they can have the things we never had. We are working on passing down houses, lands and businesses to our children not debt, stress and toxic family traits, we are focused on vibrating higher. Change your focus, change your company and the people you allow in your space, change your thinking and your mind set, refuse to allow negativity and negative people to consume you, vibrate higher. Be accountable for your own happiness and never put the keys to your happiness in someone else's pocket. Be happy with yourself and who you are, if the people around you don't like your vibes or can't accept you for who you are don't compromise your happiness to fit it, change the people you hang around. It is your happiness and you are solely responsible for it, vibrate higher, you owe it to yourself.

Chapter Fifteen

Those "V" words:
they can literally control your life

When we feel victimized, as humans our first priority is to seek revenge, we are focused on making sure that the people who hurt us pay for their perceive wrong doings. We are bitter and angry and dissatisfied: we make up in our minds that we are not going to let this go and wouldn't feel better until they get what's coming to them. We live our lives consumed with finding ways to make them pay, they must feel the pain that they made you feel or even worst. There was a time in my life when I walked in the realm of being a victim. I was constantly reeling in pain from unhealed trauma and burdened with the baggage of bitterness, anger and had my hands full of grudges and hatred. All the pain I carried around on a daily basis was excruciating, physically, mentally and emotionally crippling. I went to sleep every night and woke up every morning in mental and emotional anguish. I had plenty of pain, pain of betrayal, pain of lost, death, pain of emptiness and worthlessness, the pain of feeling unloved and unwanted, the pain of never being enough, the nightmares from my past, the unresolved, unwanted and horrific pictures that constantly played in my head. The burden of a broken parental relationship with the weight of everyone's judgment and opinions attached to it. The pain of failures at the edge of success. The pain of single parenthood and the struggle to make ends meet, I was literally and figuratively living in pain. I was living my life as a victim blaming everybody for why I couldn't succeed, finding every excuse as to why I wasn't putting my best foot forward, wallowing in self pity on a daily basis, and in some instances using it as an excuse for not trying my hardest or pushing through my tough times. Playing victim is such an easy role because it doesn't challenge you to do better. In the years I saw myself as a victim I lost much more than I gained, I had no motivation or incentive to give it my all and not only was I suffering as a result but my daughter was also suffering from some of the poor choices I made. Playing the role of victim when others are depending on you is one of the most selfish thing you can do. When you see yourself as a victim you are poised to seek vengeance. Your thought is one where if I have to suffer those people that put me in a place to endure suffering must suffer themselves. You delight when your enemies get their so called karma not realizing that because we are humans and cannot predict our futures anything can happen to us at any given time. There is an old saying "when you see your neighbor's house start washing away don't laugh at him throw sand at your doors because tomorrow it could very well be your house." In essence don't find joy when others are going through their trials and tribulations because tomorrow maybe your turn. The more you see yourself as a victim the less able you are to overcome the things of your past, and your past continues to haunt you and hamper your future. Looking back at the years I spent identifying myself as a victim and allowing that stereotype to control my life I can say I have wasted a lot of time but thankfully it is never too late to make a change for the better. In life you have to take responsibility for your own future. The wounds and trauma are not your fault but the healing is solely your responsible; if you are waiting for the people that cause your wounds to feel guilty and work with you on healing them you would be waiting your entire life. Take the responsibility for your healing into your own hands. Stop focusing on vengeance and start working on your victory. Vengeance belongs to God and only him. Stop seeing yourself as a victim and start seeing yourself as a victor.

In the realms of all the "V" words there is none more rewarding that victory. Experiencing victory from all the trauma, experiencing victory from anger, hate, grudges, emptiness, worthlessness, all the things that cause us to feel like victims. There is nothing more victorious than healing and moving on from all your past hurts. There is nothing more victorious than letting Jesus fight all your battles for you. There is nothing more powerful than walking in your victory knowing that the battles you are trying to fight isn't yours and wasn't your in the first place. There is nothing more victorious than letting go and letting God. There is nothing more victorious than finding your place of peace, a place where you can smile through your storms because you understand that those storms are nothing compare to the rainbow behind those clouds. Victory can't look the same for everybody because we are all going in different directions. I have learnt in life even things we sometimes conceive as set backs are setting us up for our victories to come. God had to take us through Egypt so he can prepare us for our journey through Canaan and to our ultimate victory of our promised land, our place to call home. When I look back on my life I am thankful for my set backs, I am thankful for my hardships and my pain, I am thankful for the days the almighty took me through the fire, the days my faith was tested; everything in life don't matter how tragic it may be is preparing us for our victory. I am no longer a victim I am a victor, I no longer seek vengeance and wait to witness the downfalls of my perceive enemies, I have emerged victorious and I walk in my purpose. Once you know what it feels like to be victorious you will no longer consider yourself a victim but an overcomer knowing that when you have a relationship with God all things are possible. When you are in pain, pray through your pain, talk to the great physician he is the greatest healer that ever lived. When you feel victimized reach into your soul and find your strength, do whatever you have to do to heal from your emotional and mental wounds, the greatest revenge is to heal and move on, tomorrow is always a better day.

Chapter Sixteen

My journey to a post-graduate degree

It is August 2018 and I am on my way back to Tyler, Texas from Chicago, Illinois after attending the graduation ceremony for my master's degree. I had spent the last two years working on completing the requirements to obtain my master's degree and it was finally over. The next few I spent my time working on the job and researching jobs that I could work in to utilize my new degree as a nurse educator. I applied for and was hired by Chamberlain University as a clinical instructor in their BSN program in Jacksonville, Florida where I was residing at the time. After my thirteen-week travel nurse assignment concluded I headed back to Jacksonville to begin my new job at Chamberlain University. During my last four weeks in Tyler, I applied for and was accepted into the doctoral program at Chamberlain University. In November 2018 I began my first class on the journey to obtaining my post-graduate degree. The next two years can be characterized as a roller coaster ride full of unpredictable twists and turns. The next three years were spent conducting research, collecting data, and working on my clinical practice change project. The days were long and laborious and nightly sleep was down to three or four hours a night. Most days I am too tired to cook so I eat fast food, and some days only eat one meal. To say I was constantly fatigued would be an understatement. I would listen to the stories told by my mentor and other colleagues who had completed their doctorate and it scared me. I spent many months in limbo between quitting because I wasn't going to make it to the next course and keeping going you can do anything you put your mind to do. Many nights I was putting the final touches on my assignment and submitting it within minutes of the 1 AM deadline; other nights I would fall asleep on the couch in the living room, too tired to climb the stairs to get to my bedroom. As a single parent, it was even more challenging because I still had to take care of my daughter and help with homework various school tasks, and after-school activities. I had bitten off more than I could chew and it was evident. In the second year of the program, I started to have chronic headaches and pain in the back of my neck; my PCP diagnosed me with tension headaches, gave me some medications, and told me that I needed to get more sleep. Rest for me was a foreign word, I would push my body to the limit until I couldn't go anymore and I would crash. In January 2020, we moved from Jacksonville, Florida to Richmond Hill, Georgia and I was driving two-plus hours each way to go on campus to teach. About two months after moving the covid pandemic was in full effect and our classes all went onto a virtual learning platform. I was teaching from home and continuing to work on my clinical practice change project to graduate.

It is August 2020, it is the final 10 weeks and final course of my doctoral program. I am tirelessly working to put the final touches on my project for IRB approval and to get my approval to graduate. We are in week 6 and we have to submit our project for review to the IRB board and the Dean of the doctoral program by the end of the week. It is Sunday night and I am nervously uploading my project to the assignment portal. It would take three days to get the school's decision on my project. It is Tuesday morning of week 7 and this morning I am not feeling well I have a headache, body aches and chills, I tried to get out of bed and was feeling very weak. As the day progressed I began to feel much worse, I spent the entire day lying in bed. The next day would be the day I find out what the University's decision on my project. It's Wednesday morning and I am lying in bed with a fever, headache, vomiting, and diarrhea; I am feeling horrible, and in addition, my anxiety is sky high as I wait for the decision on my project this was the moment of truth, after two years of sacrifice it has come down to this moment. It was after 4 PM that afternoon when the dreaded email finally came to my mailbox. I reluctantly opened it and this is what it said "Dear Maxine D'Andrade, unfortunately, the graduating body cannot approve your final project, please make the necessary corrections recommended and resubmit by the end of the week approval. My heart sank, I was battling COVID and feeling sick, helpless, and defeated; I had worked so hard, but this was not the response I was expecting. For the next few days, I spent most of my time in bed recovering, still trying to digest the bad news I had received from Chamberlain. I spent those days convincing myself that I didn't need a post-graduate degree, I had a good job, my bills were paid, I had a roof over my head, all was well, and a doctoral degree was not necessary. I didn't turn the computer on or log into the assignment portal to attempt to make the necessary changes to my project so that it could be approved, I was done. At the end of the week, I had my weekly advisement meeting with my professor and the news was even more discouraging. She told me that my project required extensive corrections to get approval for graduation and she didn't think I could do it in the short space of time and that I should request a three-month COVID withdrawal, work on my project during those three months, and come back to complete my degree. This was Friday afternoon and the paperwork for the COVID withdrawal had to be submitted by 9 Am Monday otherwise I risked failing the class and getting an F which would cause me to permanently fail out of the program. After that discussion with my professor, my mind was made up, I was quitting, I wasn't even going to formally withdraw, I was just going to drop out. The weekend came and I was feeling better physically but mentally I didn't have any fight left in me. I told Michael what my professor said and then proceeded to call my mentor I had to break the bad news. I could hear the disappointment in my mentor's voice she had worked so hard with me on this project over the past two years and now the finish line was close but yet so far away. It was Monday at 9 AM, and I did not submit the withdrawal paperwork I had already resolved in my mind that I had failed out of the program and that was it. I spent the entire day Monday ignoring calls from the professor and the registrar's office I didn't want to speak to anybody, I had convinced myself that I didn't need a post-graduate degree; I was idly lying around trying very hard to be content with not finishing the program, the devil finds work for idle minds. Tuesday came and I spent most of the day in bed until Michael came home from work. I could hear his footsteps coming towards me in the bed, I had my head under the covers but I knew he was close to me because I couldn't hear his footsteps anymore, after that I heard his voice, "Babe what's going on with your project, how far have you gone with the correction?" I told him I was not going to do anything more with the project, I had already wasted almost two years of my life on this and didn't Have any more time to waste. Michael then took the covers off me and said "Get up, let's go upstairs to your office and get the corrections done, I will not allow you to quit, you have sacrificed so much, stop this nonsense." I was reluctant but he wasn't giving up so I eventually got and we went to my office, turned the computer on, and logged into the assignment portal. For the next four days, we worked relentlessly to get the corrections done that were needed. I did the additional research, collected the required data and Mike typed, proofread, and pushed the project through Grammarly. It was Sunday and for the last four days we had stayed up late every night working on my project, we pushed it through Grammarly one final time and then uploaded it to the assignment portal. This was the moment of truth, there was no turning back I had no wiggle room, I could no longer ask for a withdrawal because the deadline had passed it was either sink or swim, pass or fail out of the program; now that the final version of my project was uploaded to the assignment portal I had to wait three days for the final decision, those were three of the most agonizing days of my life. I spent the next three days trying my best to stay positive, I was hoping for the best but also preparing for the worst. I was trying to figure out in the worst-case scenario what I would say to my students, colleagues, close friends, and family who had been there for and supported me throughout this journey but most importantly what I would say to my daughter. Those were the longest three days of my life, I stayed up because I was so anxious I couldn't fall asleep, I had lost my appetite being sick with COVID-19 and this situation made it much worse. I wanted the three to come to an end but at the same time, I wished that time would stand still because my heart wasn't ready to accept bad news. Wednesday finally came and I spent most of the day going back and forth to the restroom, my nerves were getting the best of me. It was 5:15 PM when the email finally came from Chamberlain University. I went to my office and sat in front of the computer for a few minutes before opening the email my heart was pounding and my hands were trembling as I clicked on the email to open it. The email read, "Dear Maxine D'Andrade we are pleased to inform you that you have met all the criteria and are approved for graduation." I sat there in silence for a while looking at the email, my project was approved and I was graduating, it felt surreal, and I had to pinch myself.

After a few minutes I picked up my phone and texted Mike to come upstairs he had to read this email for himself; when he got upstairs I just pointed to the computer screen, and I couldn't speak. Mike looked at me and said, "Babe you did it, I told you that you would." I looked at him and said no babe we did it this is your degree as well I couldn't do it without you, you believed in me even when I doubted myself. After that, I started calling all the people who supported me throughout this journey to break the good news, despite all the setbacks I had finally crossed the final line. My mother's prayers, my mentor's support, my husband's determination, all the support I received from close friends and family, and all my sacrifices and hard work in the last two years had finally borne fruit, it was the end of this chapter in my life. I had fought and won another battle in my life, it was the dawning of a new day. When you are at your weakest and feel like giving up that's the time you have to reach for your inner strength; you have to continue cutting through the dark clouds to get to your silver lining. When you are down on your knees and struggling to get back up pray to God for strength and keep going. You are not defeated until you stop trying, it isn't over until it's over, keep fighting. Fight, win, and live to tell your story, you may just be an inspiration to the next person task with the same or a similar battle. Respect and honor your path, trust God, and with each step you take trust your journey, learn, grow, and evolve; believe that whatever you put your mind to you can achieve, you can become anything once you continue to fight and never give up.

Chapter Seventeen

When Two Become One

It is Monday, December 25th, 2023, Christmas morning. The smell of pepperpot is in the air, we are in Guyana, South America. Today we are not only celebrating the birth of Jesus Christ but we are also celebrating our love story; today our family and close friends are gathering to celebrate with us, it is our wedding day. Some months ago I got married to my best friend and today is the day the world will be officially introduced to Mr and Mrs Elm. It was also a symbolic day for me because five years ago on this very day, I embarked on my journey of self-discovery; there was so much to celebrate on this day. I was up early but still lying in bed, I had to have my morning conversation with God before I got busy with the day's events. I said Lord this is the day that you made, I will rejoice and be glad in it. Today, you woke me up and I am privileged not only to celebrate your son's birthday but celebrate love, let this day be a true reflection of love, let the atmosphere be peaceful, and let there be love and unity, amen. I was at the table having Christmas breakfast with my husband, daughter, and my in-laws who came to Guyana to celebrate with us. I was eating my pepperpot and bread and my thoughts went back to the day I met my husband and through the next five years of our relationship, God blessed me with a good husband.

In life, you will meet different types of men and they will serve different purposes in your life; some men will break you, some will string you along until you get tired and leave, some will break and damage you emotionally and mentally, and others will be a complete waste of your time. Then, when you least expect it God will send a man that will change your life forever, for the better., this man will allow you to live your best life. My husband and I are opposites yet like pieces to a puzzle, we fit perfectly together. He is the husband that every woman dreams, hopes, and prays for. He is an excellent father, a great role model, and an inspiration to anyone he comes in contact with. When I met my husband I was still broken and damaged from all the failed relationships I had in the past but he accepted me as I was, looked beyond all my faults, and saw the good in me, he never judged me by my past, he only cared about the here and now, he taught me the importance of living in the present. We are humans so some of our mannerisms and approach to situations are different, but despite our differences, if I had to choose I would marry my husband again. We are two completely different people but we walk in oneness. Now, let's fast forward to Christmas day, 2023, and our celebration of love.

The day was well spent; there is nothing better than spending quality time with the people that you love. One of the most important takeaways from that day was the admonishment from pastor Charles to love and take care of your spouse; listen to your spouse and tune out all the other noises of the world. Meeting, dating, and marrying my husband was God answering my prayers. Through all the failed relationships, heartaches, and pain, God was teaching me lessons in preparation for the blessing he was about to bestow upon me. The love I continue to experience with my husband makes me realize that I had to go through everything that I went through to be able to recognize and appreciate true, unconditional love when it came. I sat through all the well wishes from family and friends and thought Lord you continue to bless me much more than I deserve and I don't have enough words to thank you. After the well wishes concluded we got up to dance our first dance to Eric Roberson's "Lessons" Every single word in that song was representative of my thoughts and feelings, I was telling my life story through him, I was living in the moment, and it felt like an eternity. "God has a funny way of showing you lessons, for years I would stare up in the skies with so many questions. Like, will find someone for me, or even if I'm standing in the place I need to be? I can't say that every love affair I had was perfect but every painful day and late night was worth it. Now I realize that everyone that let me down led me to you. All them sleepless nights, all the heartbreak I had led me to you. If I never went through it, I would never found a love like you. It's not about the past it is all about the present. I thought love wasn't meant to be until I felt it from you. You gave so much to me, can't help but give it back to you. Right now I just wanna breathe it, see it, and live it." (Abstract from Eric, Roberson, "Lessons").

When you receive unconditional love it becomes effortless to reciprocate it. If you are in a relationship where you don't feel respected, loved, or appreciated, walk away; trust God that when the time is right he will supply your every need according to his riches in glory. God knows what you deserve and he will bestow it upon you. Don't get comfortable and settle in dead-end relationships, you deserve to be respected, loved, and appreciated, don't accept anything less. Don't settle for cheating, lying, disrespectful men, and don't believe the myth that all men are the same. Divorce is ok, walking away from narcissistic, toxic, controlling men is ok, and not staying in verbally and physically abusive relationships because of the children is also ok. Breaking family traditions and norms and not staying married because your family looks down on divorce is acceptable; this is your life and your happiness is at stake. Pray about your decisions, ask the almighty to guide your steps, and run like your life depends on it because it does. You cannot walk in oneness with someone going in the opposite direction, you will never reach your destination or find true love. Every time you settle you fail to live out God's purpose in your life. God's desire is not for us to have just any spouse, but to have the spouse that's truly best for us. Every man isn't marriage material, if he can't respect, protect, provide, defend, love, and appreciate you, let him go he needs to remain single until he grows up; it is not your responsibility to raise or try to change a grown man, we don't date or marry our children. Don't waste your time trying to teach a grown man how he should act and who he should be; if he can't give you what you need then he is not the right man for you, you don't have to tolerate or accept mediocrity. The goal is not to marry perfect men because none of us are perfect but our husbands should be mature, respectful, trustworthy men with good characters. Women shouldn't have to worry about their men embarrassing them because they are flirtatious with wondering eyes.

When two become one and your hearts and lives are in sync there is no limit to the things you can achieve, the joy and happiness you can experience. There is no feeling more fulfilling than going to bed every night knowing that you are loved, appreciated, and protected. You wake up every day ready to face the adventures of the new day because you have God and your spouse routing for you. When two become one those mountains become mold hills, those obstacles become stepping stones, the impossibles become possible, and even the storms begin to feel like raindrops. It is one thing to dream about unconditional love but to experience it is another level of gratification. Nobody, and I mean absolutely nobody in this world goes through more pain and heartbreak than a good woman fighting to prove her love to the wrong man. Stay single, level up, and don't ever settle, vibrate higher and when the time is right God will send you the man that's truly right for you, he will send you your Boaz.

Chapter Eighteen

A place to call to home

When the time is right, I the lord will make it happen. It doesn't matter what we have done, how many poor choices we have made, or how many times we fall, God is still in the blessing business, I am living testimony. It was January 2020 when I moved from Jacksonville, Florida to Richmond Hill, Georgia a small town about twenty minutes outside of Savannah. I had no relatives or friends nearby and it was another quest to find a place to call home. The first year in Richmond Hill was a period of adjustment, the pandemic was in full force and death was everywhere, every day the news was filled with gloom and doom, I was praying every day for death not to hit my household or any close friend or family member. My daughter was going to school online and we stayed in the house except for when we had to venture out to get groceries or attend doctor's appointments and relevant things. I was teaching virtually and working on my post-graduate degree.

Mike was still working outside of the home and every day he left I would pray to God that he didn't get ill because he was the main bread-winner and as the head of the household we needed him to be safe. Despite all the turmoil that was going on in the outside world there was a sense of peace in my home. We cooked, ate, played cards, and celebrated still being alive every day. Our bond became stronger and we valued our family members and time much more. I was in a peace-ful place in my life, I was happy and had peace of mind. My daughter was happy and doing well in school. This is home, I had finally found a place to call home; not just a physical structure with food, electricity, and running water but my safe place. Don't matter where we roam, we all need a place that we can call home. For the last twenty-plus years after leaving Guyana, I embarked on a journey to find a place to call home, that journey led me in different directions and various desti-nations in search of happiness, peace, peace of mind, and a place that would be truly home physically and figuratively. Throughout those years through my struggles, failures, pain, and heartbreaks I always had a house to live in but I never found a place to call home.

Over the years I lived in five different states and each time I packed up and moved to a new state or city I hoped that I would finally find home, my happy place, my sanctuary, my place of peace, my Utopia. I wasn't looking for a big, fancy house filled with luxury and all the finer things in life, I was looking for a place where I could bloom and flourish, a place where I could be myself without judgment or stipulations, a place where the foundation was built on love and un-derstanding; a place where when life throws me lemons I could make lemonade and even add sugar to it, a place to call home in all of its true meaning. One day while I was working in home health I pulled up in a patient's driveway to complete a visit. The patient's husband was sitting in his car in the driveway when I arrived. I greeted him and made my way into the house to complete my visit with his wife. The visit concluded after about 45 minutes and I headed back to my car. The patient's husband was still sitting in his car and he wind down the window of his car while I was going back to my car and said, "Can you tell me what kind of mood my wife was in during your visit?" I smiled and told him that she was in good spirits and asked him why he was asking that question, he said, "Most days when I come home, I have to sit in my car for a while, and mentally prepare myself because she is always in a bad mood and ready to start a fight, I think she needs more psychiatric help than she needs home health." This couple was wealthy and living in one of the richer neighborhoods on a waterfront property; when you entered their house it was posh, well put together with all the luxurious things you could imagine, there were expensive cars parked in their driveway and from the outside looking in everything looked perfect. To a stranger, this would be a picture-perfect life and home but the reality was that the house was perfect but the home was broken. In life wealth, mansions, expensive cars, and owning luxurious possessions are all associated with happiness and fulfillment but sometimes some of the saddest, most miserable people you will ever meet live in those houses and drive those expensive cars. Every time there is news of a celebrity that commits suicide people lament about how rich they were and question how somebody so rich and popular could commit such a horrible act; but the truth is money can't buy happiness, joy, peace, or peace of mind, it is like a bandage that you place over a wound, it does not heal the wound or stop it from bleeding internally it is a very superficial temporary fix to a much deeper, unresolved issue. At one point in my life, my goal was to make enough money so that I could be happy and not have to worry about my bills, then the time came when I was financially stable and not worrying about my bills, I had everything I thought I needed but I still wasn't happy, had no peace of mind and still felt like something was missing. I was going to my physical house every day but it did not feel like home; I was still longing for a place to call home, a place where I was at peace with myself and others, my sanctuary, a place of tranquility. It took over twenty years for me to realize that the place I was searching for lived within me my entire life. My happy place is within me, my mind is my sanctuary, home is wherever the heart and soul are. I had lost control of my life and destiny for all these years and the only way to find a place to call home was to take back control of my life. I had to get right with God and myself, I had to love and respect myself and find my place of belonging. I had to control my thoughts and actions; I had to be mindful of the people and things that I allow to rent space in my head and disturb my peace and peace of mind, I had to prioritize my peace. There is no better gratification than finding and living in your peace, in your happy place where you no longer allow negativity to invade and destroy your home and your sanity, a place protected from all the evil of this wicked world. Home sweet home, there is no place like home, what a wonderful feeling when you finally find a place to call home, that place you longed for your entire life. There is peace like a river in my soul everyday, I have a happiness that no situation, person or circumstance can compromise or complicate; I have been set free by the almighty and I am free indeed. Free to be unapologetically me. Free to live my life on my own terms and not worry about the opinion of others, free to love and be loved, free to live everyday as if it was my last day and not have any regrets, free from my past, free from the guilt of my mistakes, free to continue on my life's journey without looking back with disappointments and dissatisfaction, only glancing back periodically to mesmerize on how far God has brought me. Free, free, free, thank God at last I am free.

Chapter Nineteen

The conclusion of the matter
- "It is well with my soul"

Self evolution is personal and everyone's journey is unique and individualized; none of us will walk the same path or embark on the same journey. We will experience growth at different stages and different paces. We should never compare our journey with anyone else because we are all destine to experience growth at our own pace. Focus on your own well being, concentrate on improving yourself, don't chase people or opportunities, focus on your growth and the right people and opportunities will find you. Our faith have to be stronger than our fears and we have to resolve in our minds to trust God where we cannot trace him, even faith like a mustard seed is enough to propel us to the next level. When we are at our lowest point and in our darkest hour our faith will guide us to the rainbow on the other side. In life it is not what you have but who you have by your side that is most important; the people who stand by your side through your failures as well as your triumphs. The people who love you in spite of your shortcomings and imperfection, the people who remain in the judgement free zone; those who accept you for who you are and not try to change you into who they feel you must be. Surround yourself with people who can add to your growth intellectually, spiritually, mentally and morally; if there are people in your life that does not contribute to your growth or embrace your journey let them go, irrespective of who they are, the greatest burden of weight that you can carry around is the weight of other people's negativity. Disassociate yourself from people who see you as competition rather than a person trying everyday to fulfill his or her God given purpose. People who sees you as competition will never support you their only reason for being around you is to make sure that they are present when you fail. Learn how to move on from people and things that don't serve you well, find your journey, respect your journey and walk in it. Love yourself, respect how far you have come and don't let anyone use your past against you; most importantly don't let your past hinder you from your future, don't let it become a life sentence. Learn to be your biggest competitor, strive everyday to be a better person than the person you were the day before, clap for yourself there is nothing wrong with tooting your own horn after you have worked hard and achieved your goals. Celebrate you and your milestones, you have come a long way despite your troubled waters. Be proud of where you came from and be even more proud of where you are going, most of us came from humble beginnings and despite not being born with golden spoons in our mouths we have achieve successes on many levels.

Life is short, today or tomorrow is not promised to any of us, some of us wake up in the morning and die before the day is over, others go to sleep at night and never wake up to see the next morning. Time is precious, we cannot retrieve wasted time. If we lose money we can always replenish it but if we lose time it is lost forever. Live each day of your life with purpose and gratitude, don't waste time murmuring about the things you don't have instead appreciate and be thankful for the things you do have. Be thankful that you are still counted among the living and still have the opportunity to change the things you don't like and to make today a fulfilling one. Don't allow your soul to be so consumed with the ill wills of yesterday that you leave no space for the blessings of today. Everyday that you wake up find something to be thankful for; God promise to bless us abundantly but we fail to claim those blessings because we spend too much time lamenting about all the things in our lives that are wrong instead of being thankful and allowing God to continue to bestow blessings upon us. We need to get into the habit of counting our blessings instead of counting our Trials and tribulations and wallowing in self-pity. When I say count your blessings I am not referring to material things, I am speaking about the blessings of peace, tranquility, contentment, of a sane mind, that peace that passeth all understanding. When Job lost everything he had, everybody expected him to lose faith, curse God and die but because Job understood that his blessings were not measured by the material things he had or how wealthy he was he was at peace and still praising God because he knew that greater was he that was in him than he that was in the world, Job understood the assignment; that is the beauty of trusting God when you cannot trace him. Job's response to losing all his earthly belongings is the beauty of knowing that the Lord giveth, he taketh away and he restore. Think about Job one minute losing everything, skin covered with sores, pushed to the brink of death and the next minute receiving more blessings than he could ever imagined, our God is more than able. When our faith is tested and we endure trials and tribulations God is preparing us for greater things to come. When our blessings seems to be delayed the almighty is teaching us patience so that we can appreciate our blessings when he bestow them upon us. God works in mysterious ways and his timing is the best timing, there is a reason for everything we go through in life even those things that we struggle to understand. When the odds are against us and we feel hopeless and our faith begins to waiver that is the time we have to seek out and find God, lean upon him and know that through it all he will never leave us nor forsake us, he is the beacon of light that guides us as we walk through the valleys of the shadows of death. The almighty is our way maker, the solid rock on which we must place all our troubles, even in our tears he understands and is with us. We have to trust our unknown future to an all knowing God he knows it all and will always lift us up out of all our storms. When we feel like we are drowning, we can't walk on water but he certainly can, we just need to place all our burdens, sorrows, trials and tribulations at the foot of the cross and let him who holds the weight of the world in his hands carry them for us. Tomorrow is always a brighter day, and despite what we are facing when we have the almighty with us we can say like the psalmist, "it is well, it is well with my soul."

Printed by Libri Plureos GmbH in Hamburg,
Germany